C# 4.0
Pocket Reference

THIRD EDITION

C# 4.0
Pocket Reference

Joseph Albahari and Ben Albahari

Beijing · Cambridge · Farnham · Köln · Sebastopol · Tokyo

C# 4.0 Pocket Reference, Third Edition
by Joseph Albahari and Ben Albahari

Published by O'Reilly Media, Inc., 1005 Gravenstein Highway North, Sebastopol, CA 95472.

O'Reilly books may be purchased for educational, business, or sales promotional use. Online editions are also available for most titles (*http://my.safari booksonline.com*). For more information, contact our corporate/institutional sales department: (800) 998-9938 or *corporate@oreilly.com*.

Editor: Mike Hendrickson
Production Editor: Kristen Borg
Proofreader: Kiel Van Horn
Indexer: Angela Howard
Cover Designer: Karen Montgomery
Interior Designer: David Futato
Illustrator: Robert Romano

Printing History:

November 2002:	First Edition.
February 2008:	Second Edition.
August 2010:	Third Edition.

ISBN: 978-1-449-39401-1

[TM]   [2011-04-01]

1301624430

Contents

C# 4.0 Pocket Reference

C# is a general-purpose, type-safe, object-oriented programming language whose goal is programmer productivity. To this end, the language balances simplicity, expressiveness, and performance. The C# language is platform-neutral, but it was written to work well with the Microsoft *.NET Framework*. C# 4.0 targets .NET Framework 4.0.

NOTE

The programs and code snippets in this book mirror those in Chapters 2–4 of *C# 4.0 in a Nutshell* (Joseph and Ben Albahari, O'Reilly) and are all available as interactive samples in LINQPad. Working through these samples in conjunction with the book accelerates learning, in that you can edit the samples and instantly see the results without needing to set up projects and solutions in Visual Studio.

To download the samples, click the *Samples* tab in LINQPad and click "Download more samples." LINQPad is free—go to *http://www.linqpad.net*.

Using Code Examples

This book is here to help you get your job done. In general, you may use the code in this book in your programs and documentation. You do not need to contact us for permission unless you're reproducing a significant portion of the code. For example, writing a program that uses several chunks of code from this book does not require permission. Selling or distributing a CD-ROM of examples from O'Reilly books does require permission. Answering a question by citing this book and quoting example code does not require permission. Incorporating a significant amount of example code from this book into your product's documentation does require permission.

We appreciate, but do not require, attribution. An attribution usually includes the title, author, publisher, and ISBN. For example: "*C# 4.0 Pocket Reference*, Third Edition, by Joseph Albahari and Ben Albahari. Copyright 2010 Joseph Albahari and Ben Albahari, 978-1-449-39401-1."

If you feel that your use of code examples falls outside of fair use or the permission given here, feel free to contact us at *permissions@oreilly.com*.

How to Contact Us

Please address comments and questions concerning this book to the publisher:

O'Reilly Media, Inc.
1005 Gravenstein Highway North
Sebastopol, CA 95472
800-998-9938 (in the United States or Canada)
707-829-0515 (international or local)
707-829-0104 (fax)

We have a web page for this book, where we list errata, examples, and additional information. You can access this page at:

http://oreilly.com/catalog/0636920013365/

To comment or ask technical questions about this book, send email to:

bookquestions@oreilly.com

For more information about our books, conferences, Resource Centers, and the O'Reilly Network, see our website at:

http://oreilly.com

Safari® Books Online

Safari Books Online is an on-demand digital library that lets you easily search over 7,500 technology and creative reference books and videos to find the answers you need quickly.

With a subscription, you can read any page and watch any video from our library online. Read books on your cell phone and mobile devices. Access new titles before they are available for print, and get exclusive access to manuscripts in development and post feedback for the authors. Copy and paste code samples, organize your favorites, download chapters, bookmark key sections, create notes, print out pages, and benefit from tons of other time-saving features.

O'Reilly Media has uploaded this book to the Safari Books Online service. To have full digital access to this book and others on similar topics from O'Reilly and other publishers, sign up for free at *http://my.safaribooksonline.com*.

A First C# Program

Here is a program that multiplies 12 by 30, and prints the result, 360, to the screen. The double forward slashes indicate that the remainder of a line is a *comment*:

```
using System;                    // Importing namespace
```

```
class Test                    // Class declaration
{
  static void Main()          // Method declaration
  {
    int x = 12 * 30;          // Statement 1
    Console.WriteLine (x);    // Statement 2
  }                           // End of method
}                             // End of class
```

At the heart of this program lies two *statements*. Statements in
C# execute sequentially. Each statement is terminated by a
semicolon. The first statement computes the *expression*
12 * 30 and stores the result in a *local variable*, named x, which
is an integer type. The second statement calls the Console
class's WriteLine *method*, to print the variable x to a text win-
dow on the screen.

A *method* performs an action in a series of statements, called a
statement block—a pair of braces containing zero or more
statements. We defined a single method named Main.

Writing higher-level functions that call upon lower-level functions simplifies a program. We can *refactor* our program with
a reusable method that multiplies an integer by 12, as follows:

```
using System;

class Test
{
  static void Main()
  {
    Console.WriteLine (FeetToInches (30));    // 360
    Console.WriteLine (FeetToInches (100));   // 1200
  }

  static int FeetToInches (int feet)
  {
    int inches = feet * 12;
    return inches;
  }
}
```

A method can receive *input* data from the caller by specifying
parameters and *output* data back to the caller by specifying a
return type. We defined a method called FeetToInches that has

---

a parameter for inputting feet, and a return type for outputting inches, both of type **int** (integer).

The *literals* 30 and 100 are the *arguments* passed to the **Feet ToInches** method. The **Main** method in our example has empty parentheses because it has no parameters, and is **void** because it doesn't return any value to its caller. C# recognizes a method called **Main** as signaling the default entry point of execution. The **Main** method may optionally return an integer (rather than **void**) in order to return a value to the execution environment. The **Main** method can also optionally accept an array of strings as a parameter (that will be populated with any arguments passed to the executable). For example:

```
static int Main (string[] args) {...}
```

NOTE

An array (such as **string[]**) represents a fixed number of elements of a particular type (see the section "Arrays" on page 31).

Methods are one of several kinds of functions in C#. Another kind of function we used was the * *operator*, to perform multiplication. There are also *constructors*, *properties*, *events*, *indexers*, and *finalizers*.

In our example, the two methods are grouped into a class. A *class* groups function members and data members to form an object-oriented building block. The **Console** class groups members that handle command-line input/output functionality, such as the **WriteLine** method. Our **Test** class groups two methods—the **Main** method and the **FeetToInches** method. A class is a kind of *type*, which we will examine in "Type Basics" on page 10.

At the outermost level of a program, types are organized into *namespaces*. The **using** directive was used to make the **System** namespace available to our application, to use the **Console** class. We could define all our classes within the `TestPrograms` namespace, as follows:

```
using System;

namespace TestPrograms
{
  class Test  {...}
  class Test2 {...}
}
```

The .NET Framework is organized into nested namespaces. For example, this is the namespace that contains types for handling text:

```
using System.Text;
```

The **using** directive is there for convenience; you can also refer to a type by its fully qualified name, which is the type name prefixed with its namespace, such as `System.Text.String Builder`.

Compilation

The C# compiler compiles source code, specified as a set of files with the *.cs* extension, into an *assembly*. An assembly is the unit of packaging and deployment in .NET. An assembly can be either an *application* or a *library*. A normal console or Windows application has a **Main** method and is an *.exe* file. A library is a *.dll* and is equivalent to an *.exe* without an entry point. Its purpose is to be called upon (*referenced*) by an application or by other libraries. The .NET Framework is a set of libraries.

The name of the C# compiler is *csc.exe*. You can either use an IDE such as Visual Studio to compile, or call **csc** manually from the command line. To compile manually, first save a program to a file such as *MyFirstProgram.cs*, and then go to the command line and invoke **csc** (located under *%SystemRoot% \Microsoft.NET\Framework\<framework-version>*, where *%SystemRoot%* is your Windows directory) as follows:

```
csc MyFirstProgram.cs
```

This produces an application named *MyFirstProgram.exe*.

To produce a library (*.dll*), do the following:

```
csc /target:library MyFirstProgram.cs
```

Syntax

C# syntax is based on C and C++ syntax. In this section, we will describe C#'s elements of syntax, using the following program:

```
using System;

class Test
{
  static void Main()
  {
    int x = 12 * 30;
    Console.WriteLine (x);
  }
}
```

Identifiers and Keywords

Identifiers are names that programmers choose for their classes, methods, variables, and so on. These are the identifiers in our example program, in the order they appear:

```
System   Test   Main   x   Console   WriteLine
```

An identifier must be a whole word, essentially made up of Unicode characters starting with a letter or underscore. C# identifiers are case-sensitive. By convention, parameters, local variables, and private fields should be in camel case (e.g., myVariable), and all other identifiers should be in Pascal case (e.g., MyMethod).

Keywords are names reserved by the compiler that you can't use as identifiers. These are the keywords in our example program:

```
using   class   static   void   int
```

Here is the full list of C# keywords:

abstract	enum	long	stackalloc
as	event	namespace	static
base	explicit	new	string
bool	extern	null	struct
break	false	object	switch
byte	finally	operator	this
case	fixed	out	throw
catch	float	override	true
char	for	params	try
checked	foreach	private	typeof
class	goto	protected	uint
const	if	public	ulong
continue	implicit	readonly	unchecked
decimal	in	ref	unsafe
default	int	return	ushort
delegate	interface	sbyte	using
do	internal	sealed	virtual
double	is	short	void
else	lock	sizeof	while

Avoiding conflicts

If you really want to use an identifier that clashes with a keyword, you can do so by qualifying it with the @ prefix. For instance:

```
class class  {...}     // Illegal
class @class {...}     // Legal
```

The @ symbol doesn't form part of the identifier itself. So @myVariable is the same as myVariable.

Contextual keywords

Some keywords are *contextual*, meaning they can also be used as identifiers—without an @ symbol. These are:

add	from	join	select
ascending	get	let	set
by	global	on	value
descending	group	orderby	var
dynamic	in	partial	where
equals	into	remove	yield

With contextual keywords, ambiguity cannot arise within the context in which they are used.

Literals, Punctuators, and Operators

Literals are primitive pieces of data statically embedded into the program. The literals in our example program are 12 and 30. *Punctuators* help demarcate the structure of the program. The punctuators in our program are, ;, {, and }.

The semicolon terminates a statement. Statements can wrap multiple lines:

```
Console.WriteLine
    (1 + 2 + 3 + 4 + 5 + 6 + 7 + 8 + 9 + 10);
```

The braces group multiple statements into a statement block.

An *operator* transforms and combines expressions. Most operators in C# are denoted with a symbol, such as the multiplication operator, *. The operators in our program are:

```
.   ()   *   =
```

The period denotes a member of something (or a decimal point with numeric literals). The parentheses are used when declaring or calling a method; empty parentheses are used when the method accepts no arguments. The equals sign is used for *assignment* (the double equals signs, ==, are used for equality comparison).

Comments

C# offers two different styles of source-code documentation: *single-line comments* and *multiline comments*. A single-line comment begins with a double forward slash and continues until the end of the line. For example:

```
int x = 3;   // Comment about assigning 3 to x
```

A multiline comment begins with /* and ends with */. For example:

```
int x = 3;   /* This is a comment that
                spans two lines */
```

Comments may embed XML documentation tags (see "XML Documentation" on page 184).

Type Basics

A *type* defines the blueprint for a value. A *value* is a storage location denoted by a *variable* (if it can change) or a *constant* (if it cannot). We created a local variable named x in our first program.

All values in C# are an *instance* of a specific type. The meaning of a value, and the set of possible values a variable can have, is determined by its type. The type of x in our example program is int.

Predefined Type Examples

Predefined types (also called built-in types) are types that are specially supported by the compiler. The int type is a predefined type for representing the set of integers that fit into 32 bits of memory, from -2^{31} to $2^{31}-1$. We can perform functions such as arithmetic with instances of the int type as follows:

```
int x = 12 * 30;
```

Another predefined C# type is **string**. The **string** type represents a sequence of characters, such as ".NET" or "*http://oreilly .com*". We can work with strings by calling functions on them as follows:

```
string message = "Hello world";
string upperMessage = message.ToUpper();
Console.WriteLine (upperMessage);      // HELLO WORLD

int x = 2007;
message = message + x.ToString();
Console.WriteLine (message);            // Hello world2007
```

The predefined **bool** type has exactly two possible values: **true** and **false**. The **bool** type is commonly used to conditionally branch execution flow with an **if** statement. For example:

```
bool simpleVar = false;
if (simpleVar)
  Console.WriteLine ("This will not print");

int x = 5000;
bool lessThanAMile = x < 5280;
if (lessThanAMile)
  Console.WriteLine ("This will print");
```

NOTE

The System namespace in the .NET Framework contains many important types that are not predefined by C# (e.g., DateTime).

Custom Type Examples

Just as we can build complex functions from simple functions, we can build complex types from primitive types. In this example, we will define a custom type named **UnitConverter**—a class that serves as a blueprint for unit conversions:

```
using System;
```

```
public class UnitConverter
{
  int ratio;                          // Field

  public UnitConverter (int unitRatio)   // Constructor
  {
    ratio = unitRatio;
  }

  public int Convert (int unit)          // Method
  {
    return unit * ratio;
  }
}

class Test
{
  static void Main()
  {
    UnitConverter feetToInches = new UnitConverter(12);
    UnitConverter milesToFeet = new UnitConverter(5280);

    Console.Write (feetToInches.Convert(30));    // 360
    Console.Write (feetToInches.Convert(100));   // 1200
    Console.Write (feetToInches.Convert
                     (milesToFeet.Convert(1)));   // 63360
  }
}
```

Members of a type

A type contains *data members* and *function members*. The data member of **UnitConverter** is the *field* called **ratio**. The function members of **UnitConverter** are the Convert method and the **UnitConverter**'s *constructor*.

Symmetry of predefined types and custom types

A beautiful aspect of C# is that predefined types and custom types have few differences. The predefined **int** type serves as a blueprint for integers. It holds data—32 bits—and provides function members that use that data, such as **ToString**. Similarly, our custom **UnitConverter** type acts as a blueprint for unit conversions. It holds data—the ratio—and provides function members to use that data.

Constructors and instantiation

Data is created by *instantiating* a type. Predefined types can be instantiated simply by using a literal. For example, the following line instantiates two integers (**12** and **30**), which are used to compute a third instance, **x**:

```
int x = 12 * 30;
```

The **new** operator is needed to create a new instance of a custom type. We started our **Main** method by creating two instances of the **UnitConverter** type. Immediately after the **new** operator instantiates an object, the object's *constructor* is called to perform initialization. A constructor is defined like a method, except that the method name and return type are reduced to the name of the enclosing type:

```
public UnitConverter (int unitRatio)    // Constructor
{
  ratio = unitRatio;
}
```

Instance versus static members

The data members and function members that operate on the *instance* of the type are called instance members. The **UnitConverter**'s **Convert** method and the **int**'s **ToString** method are examples of instance members. By default, members are instance members.

Data members and function members that don't operate on the instance of the type, but rather on the type itself, must be marked as **static**. The **Test.Main** and **Console.WriteLine** methods are static methods. The **Console** class is actually a *static class*, which means *all* its members are static. You never actually create instances of a **Console**—one console is shared across the whole application.

To contrast instance versus static members, the instance field Name pertains to an instance of a particular Panda, whereas Population pertains to the set of all Panda instances:

```
public class Panda
{
  public string Name;          // Instance field
  public static int Population; // Static field

  public Panda (string n)      // Constructor
  {
    Name = n;                  // Assign instance field
    Population = Population+1;  // Increment static field
  }
}
```

The following code creates two instances of the Panda, prints their names, and then prints the total population:

```
Panda p1 = new Panda ("Pan Dee");
Panda p2 = new Panda ("Pan Dah");

Console.WriteLine (p1.Name);       // Pan Dee
Console.WriteLine (p2.Name);       // Pan Dah

Console.WriteLine (Panda.Population);   // 2
```

The public keyword

The public keyword exposes members to other classes. In this example, if the Name field in Panda was not public, the Test class could not access it. Marking a member public is how a type communicates: "Here is what I want other types to see—everything else is my own private implementation details." In object-oriented terms, we say that the public members *encapsulate* the private members of the class.

Conversions

C# can convert between instances of compatible types. A conversion always creates a new value from an existing one. Conversions can be either *implicit* or *explicit*: implicit conversions happen automatically, whereas explicit conversions require a *cast*. In the following example, we *implicitly* convert an `int` to a `long` type (which has twice the bitwise capacity of an `int`) and *explicitly* cast an `int` to a `short` type (which has half the bitwise capacity of an `int`):

```
int x = 12345;        // int is a 32-bit integer
long y = x;           // Implicit conversion to 64-bit int
short z = (short)x;   // Explicit conversion to 16-bit int
```

In general, implicit conversions are allowed when the compiler can guarantee they will always succeed without loss of information. Otherwise, you must perform an explicit cast to convert between compatible types.

Value Types Versus Reference Types

C# types can be divided into *value types* and *reference types*.

Value types comprise most built-in types (specifically, all numeric types, the `char` type, and the `bool` type) as well as custom `struct` and `enum` types. *Reference types* comprise all class, array, delegate, and interface types.

The fundamental difference between value types and reference types is how they are handled in memory.

Value types

The content of a *value type* variable or constant is simply a value. For example, the content of the built-in value type, `int`, is 32 bits of data.

You can define a custom value type with the `struct` keyword (see Figure 1):

```
public struct Point { public int X, Y; }
```

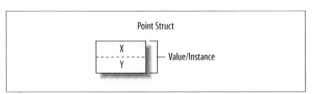

Figure 1. A value-type instance in memory

The assignment of a value-type instance always *copies* the instance. For example:

```
Point p1 = new Point();
p1.X = 7;

Point p2 = p1;              // Assignment causes copy

Console.WriteLine (p1.X);   // 7
Console.WriteLine (p2.X);   // 7

p1.X = 9;                   // Change p1.X
Console.WriteLine (p1.X);   // 9
Console.WriteLine (p2.X);   // 7
```

Figure 2 shows that **p1** and **p2** have independent storage.

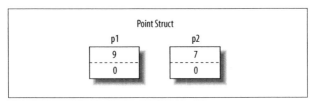

Figure 2. Assignment copies a value-type instance

Reference types

A reference type is more complex than a value type, having two parts: an *object* and the *reference* to that object. The content of a reference-type variable or constant is a reference to an object that contains the value. Here is the **Point** type from our previous example rewritten as a class (see Figure 3):

```
public class Point { public int X, Y; }
```

Assigning a reference-type variable copies the reference, not the object instance. This allows multiple variables to refer to the same object—something not ordinarily possible with value types. If we repeat the previous example, but with **Point** now a class, an operation via **p1** affects **p2**:

```
Point p1 = new Point();
p1.X = 7;
```

```
Point p2 = p1;              // Copies p1 reference

Console.WriteLine (p1.X);   // 7
Console.WriteLine (p2.X);   // 7

p1.X = 9;                   // Change p1.X
Console.WriteLine (p1.X);   // 9
Console.WriteLine (p2.X);   // 9
```

Figure 4 shows that p1 and p2 are two references that point to
the same object.

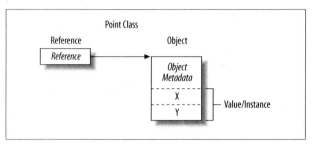

Figure 3. A reference-type instance in memory

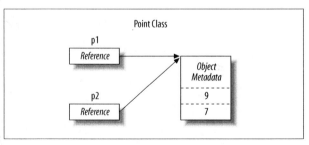

Figure 4. Assignment copies a reference

Null

A reference can be assigned the literal null, indicating that the
reference points to no object. Assuming Point is a class:

```
Point p = null;
Console.WriteLine (p == null);   // True
```

Accessing a member of a null reference generates a runtime error:

```
Console.WriteLine (p.X);   // NullReferenceException
```

In contrast, a value type cannot ordinarily have a null value:

```
struct Point {...}
...
Point p = null;  // Compile-time error
int x = null;    // Compile-time error
```

NOTE

C# has a special construct, called *nullable types*, for representing value-type nulls (see the section "Nullable Types" on page 130).

Predefined Type Taxonomy

The predefined types in C# are:

Value types

- Numeric
  - Signed integer (sbyte, short, int, long)
  - Unsigned integer (byte, ushort, uint, ulong)
  - Real number (float, double, decimal)
- Logical (bool)
- Character (char)

Reference types

- String (string)
- Object (object)

Predefined types in C# alias Framework types in the System namespace. There is only a syntactic difference between these two statements:

```
int i = 5;
System.Int32 i = 5;
```

The set of predefined *value* types, excluding **decimal**, are known as *primitive types* in the Common Language Runtime (CLR). Primitive types are so called because they are supported directly via instructions in compiled code, which usually translates to direct support on the underlying processor.

Numeric Types

C# has the following predefined numeric types:

C# type	System type	Suffix	Size	Range
Integral—signed				
sbyte	SByte		8 bits	-2^7 to 2^7-1
short	Int16		16 bits	-2^{15} to $2^{15}-1$
int	Int32		32 bits	-2^{31} to $2^{31}-1$
long	Int64	L	64 bits	-2^{63} to $2^{63}-1$
Integral—unsigned				
byte	Byte		8 bits	0 to 2^8-1
ushort	UInt16		16 bits	0 to $2^{16}-1$
uint	UInt32	U	32 bits	0 to $2^{32}-1$
ulong	UInt64	UL	64 bits	0 to $2^{64}-1$
Real				
float	Single	F	32 bits	$\pm (\sim 10^{-45}$ to $10^{38})$
double	Double	D	64 bits	$\pm (\sim 10^{-324}$ to $10^{308})$
decimal	Decimal	M	128 bits	$\pm (\sim 10^{-28}$ to $10^{28})$

Of the *integral* types, **int** and **long** are first-class citizens and are favored by both C# and the runtime. The other integral types are typically used for interoperability or when space efficiency is paramount.

Of the *real* number types, **float** and **double** are called *floating-point types* and are typically used for scientific calculations. The **decimal** type is typically used for financial calculations, where base-10-accurate arithmetic and high precision are required. (Technically, `decimal` is a floating-point type too, although it's not generally referred to as such.)

Numeric Literals

Integral literals can use decimal or hexadecimal notation; hexadecimal is denoted with the `0x` prefix (for example, `0x7f` is equivalent to `127`). *Real literals* may use decimal or exponential notation, such as `1E06`.

Numeric literal type inference

By default, the compiler *infers* a numeric literal to be either `double` or an integral type:

- If the literal contains a decimal point or the exponential symbol (`E`), it is a `double`.
- Otherwise, the literal's type is the first type in this list that can fit the literal's value: `int`, `uint`, `long`, and `ulong`.

For example:

```
Console.Write (        1.0.GetType()); // Double (double)
Console.Write (      1E06.GetType()); // Double (double)
Console.Write (         1.GetType()); // Int32  (int)
Console.Write (0xF0000000.GetType()); // UInt32 (uint)
```

Numeric suffixes

The *numeric suffixes* listed in the preceding table explicitly define the type of a literal:

```
decimal d = 3.5M;   // M = decimal (case-insensitive)
```

The suffixes U and L are rarely necessary, because the `uint`, `long`, and `ulong` types can nearly always be either *inferred* or *implicitly converted* from `int`:

```
long i = 5;      // Implicit conversion from int to long
```

The D suffix is technically redundant, in that all literals with a decimal point are inferred to be double (and you can always add a decimal point to a numeric literal). The F and M suffixes are the most useful and are mandatory when specifying fractional **float** or **decimal** literals. Without suffixes, the following would not compile, because 4.5 would be inferred to be of type **double**, which has no implicit conversion to **float** or **decimal**:

```
float f = 4.5F;        // Won't compile without suffix
decimal d = -1.23M;    // Won't compile without suffix
```

Numeric Conversions

Integral to integral conversions

Integral conversions are *implicit* when the destination type can represent every possible value of the source type. Otherwise, an *explicit* conversion is required. For example:

```
int x = 12345;         // int is a 32-bit integral
long y = x;            // Implicit conversion to 64-bit int
short z = (short)x;    // Explicit conversion to 16-bit int
```

Real to real conversions

A **float** can be implicitly converted to a **double**, since a **double** can represent every possible **float** value. The reverse conversion must be explicit.

Conversions between **decimal** and other real types must be explicit.

Real to integral conversions

Conversions from integral types to real types are implicit, whereas the reverse must be explicit. Converting from a floating-point to an integral truncates any fractional portion; to perform rounding conversions, use the static **System.Convert** class.

A caveat is that implicitly converting a large integral type to a floating-point type preserves *magnitude* but may occasionally lose *precision*:

```
int i1 = 100000001;
float f = i1;      // Magnitude preserved, precision lost
int i2 = (int)f;   // 100000000
```

Arithmetic Operators

The arithmetic operators (+, -, *, /, %) are defined for all numeric types except the 8- and 16-bit integral types. The % operator evaluates the remainder after division.

Increment and Decrement Operators

The increment and decrement operators (++, --) increment or decrement numeric types by 1. The operator can either precede or follow the variable, depending on whether you want the variable to be updated *before* or *after* the expression is evaluated. For example:

```
int x = 0;
Console.WriteLine (x++);    // Outputs 0; x is now 1
Console.WriteLine (++x);    // Outputs 2; x is now 2
Console.WriteLine (--x);    // Outputs 1; x is now 1
```

Specialized Integral Operations

Integral division

Division operations on integral types always truncate remainders. Dividing by a variable whose value is zero generates a runtime error (a DivideByZeroException). Dividing by the *literal* 0 generates a compile-time error.

Integral overflow

At runtime, arithmetic operations on integral types can overflow. By default, this happens silently—no exception is thrown. While the C# specification is agnostic as to the result of an overflow, the CLR always causes wraparound behavior. For example, decrementing the minimum possible int value results in the maximum possible int value:

```
int a = int.MinValue; a--;
Console.WriteLine (a == int.MaxValue); // True
```

The checked and unchecked operators

The checked operator tells the runtime to generate an `Over flowException` rather than failing silently when an integral expression or statement exceeds the arithmetic limits of that type. The checked operator affects expressions with the `++`, `--`, (unary) `-`, `+`, `-`, `*`, `/`, and explicit conversion operators between integral types.

checked can be used around either an expression or a statement block. For example:

```
int a = 1000000, int b = 1000000;

int c = checked (a * b);   // Checks just the expression

checked                    // Checks all expressions
{                          // in statement block.
   c = a * b;
   ...
}
```

You can make arithmetic overflow checking the default for all expressions in a program by compiling with the `/checked+` command-line switch (in Visual Studio, go to Advanced Build Settings). If you then need to disable overflow checking just for specific expressions or statements, you can do so with the unchecked operator.

Bitwise operators

C# supports the following bitwise operations:

Operator	Meaning	Sample expression	Result
~	Complement	~0xfU	0xfffffff0U
&	And	0xf0 & 0x33	0x30
|	Or	0xf0 | 0x33	0xf3
^	Exclusive Or	0xff00 ^ 0x0ff0	0xf0f0
<<	Shift left	0x20 << 2	0x80
>>	Shift right	0x20 >> 1	0x10

8- and 16-Bit Integrals

The 8- and 16-bit integral types are byte, sbyte, short, and ushort. These types lack their own arithmetic operators, so C# implicitly converts them to larger types as required. This can cause a compilation error when trying to assign the result back to a small integral type:

```
short x = 1, y = 1;
short z = x + y;          // Compile-time error
```

In this case, x and y are implicitly converted to int so that the addition can be performed. This means the result is also an int, which cannot be implicitly cast back to a short (because it could cause loss of data). To make this compile, we must add an explicit cast:

```
short z = (short) (x + y);   // OK
```

Special Float and Double Values

Unlike integral types, floating-point types have values that certain operations treat specially. These special values are NaN (Not a Number), +∞, -∞, and -0. The float and double classes have constants for NaN, +∞, and -∞ (as well as other values, including MaxValue, MinValue, and Epsilon). For example:

```
Console.Write (double.NegativeInfinity);   // -Infinity
```

Dividing a nonzero number by zero results in an infinite value:

```
Console.WriteLine ( 1.0 /  0.0);   //  Infinity
Console.WriteLine (-1.0 /  0.0);   // -Infinity
Console.WriteLine ( 1.0 / -0.0);   // -Infinity
Console.WriteLine (-1.0 / -0.0);   //  Infinity
```

Dividing zero by zero, or subtracting infinity from infinity, results in a NaN:

```
Console.Write ( 0.0 / 0.0);                //  NaN
Console.Write ((1.0 / 0.0) - (1.0 / 0.0)); //  NaN
```

When using ==, a NaN value is never equal to another value, even another NaN value. To test whether a value is NaN, you must use the float.IsNaN or double.IsNaN method:

```
Console.WriteLine (0.0 / 0.0 == double.NaN);    // False
Console.WriteLine (double.IsNaN (0.0 / 0.0));   // True
```

When using **object.Equals**, however, two NaN values are equal:

```
bool isTrue = object.Equals (0.0/0.0, double.NaN);
```

double Versus decimal

double is useful for scientific computations (such as computing spatial coordinates). **decimal** is useful for financial computations and values that are "man-made" rather than the result of real-world measurements. Here's a summary of the differences:

Feature	double	decimal
Internal representation	Base 2	Base 10
Precision	15-16 significant figures	28–29 significant figures
Range	$\pm(\sim 10^{-324}$ to $\sim 10^{308})$	$\pm(\sim 10^{-28}$ to $\sim 10^{28})$
Special values	+0, −0, +∞, −∞, and NaN	None
Speed	Native to processor	Nonnative to processor (about 10 times slower than double)

Real Number Rounding Errors

float and **double** internally represent numbers in base-2. For this reason, most literals with a fractional component (which are in base-10) will not be represented precisely:

```
float tenth = 0.1f;                      // Not quite 0.1
float one   = 1f;
Console.WriteLine (one - tenth * 10f);   // -1.490116E-08
```

This is why **float** and **double** are bad for financial calculations. In contrast, **decimal** works in base-10 and can precisely represent fractional numbers such as 0.1 (whose base-10 representation is nonrecurring).

Boolean Type and Operators

C#'s **bool** type (aliasing the `System.Boolean` type) is a logical value that can be assigned the literal **true** or **false**.

Although a Boolean value requires only one bit of storage, the runtime will use one byte of memory, since this is the minimum chunk that the runtime and processor can efficiently work with. To avoid space-inefficiency in the case of arrays, the Framework provides a `BitArray` class in the `System.Collec tions` namespace, designed to use just one bit per Boolean value.

Equality and Comparison Operators

== and != test for equality and inequality of any type, and always return a **bool** value. Value types typically have a very simple notion of equality:

```
int x = 1, y = 2, z = 1;
Console.WriteLine (x == y);      // False
Console.WriteLine (x == z);      // True
```

For reference types, equality, by default, is based on *reference*, as opposed to the actual *value* of the underlying object. Therefore, two instances of an object with identical data are not considered equal unless the == operator for that type is specially overloaded to that effect (see the section "The object Type" on page 78 and the section "Operator Overloading" on page 135).

The equality and comparison operators, ==, !=, <, >, >=, and <=, work for all numeric types, but should be used with caution with real numbers (see "Real Number Rounding Errors" on page 25 in the previous section). The comparison operators also work on **enum** type members, by comparing their underlying integral values.

Conditional Operators

The && and || operators test for *and* and *or* conditions. They are frequently used in conjunction with the ! operator, which expresses *not*. In this example, the UseUmbrella method returns true if it's rainy or sunny (to protect us from the rain or the sun), as long as it's not also windy (since umbrellas are useless in the wind):

```
static bool UseUmbrella (bool rainy, bool sunny,
                         bool windy)
{
  return !windy && (rainy || sunny);
}
```

The && and || operators *short-circuit* evaluation when possible. In the preceding example, if it is windy, the expression (rainy || sunny) is not even evaluated. Short circuiting is essential in allowing expressions such as the following to run without throwing a NullReferenceException:

```
if (sb != null && sb.Length > 0) ...
```

The & and | operators also test for *and* and *or* conditions:

```
return !windy & (rainy | sunny);
```

The difference is that they *do not short-circuit*. For this reason, they are rarely used in place of conditional operators.

The ternary conditional operator (simply called the *conditional operator*) has the form q ? a : b, where if condition q is true, a is evaluated, else b is evaluated. For example:

```
static int Max (int a, int b)
{
  return (a > b) ? a : b;
}
```

The conditional operator is particularly useful in LINQ queries.

Strings and Characters

C#'s `char` type (aliasing the `System.Char` type) represents a Unicode character and occupies two bytes. A `char` literal is specified inside single quotes:

```
char c = 'A';        // Simple character
```

Escape sequences express characters that cannot be expressed or interpreted literally. An escape sequence is a backslash followed by a character with a special meaning. For example:

```
char newLine = '\n';
char backSlash = '\\';
```

The escape sequence characters are:

Char	Meaning	Value
\'	Single quote	0x0027
\"	Double quote	0x0022
\\	Backslash	0x005C
\0	Null	0x0000
\a	Alert	0x0007
\b	Backspace	0x0008
\f	Form feed	0x000C
\n	New line	0x000A
\r	Carriage return	0x000D
\t	Horizontal tab	0x0009
\v	Vertical tab	0x000B

The `\u` (or `\x`) escape sequence lets you specify any Unicode character via its four-digit hexadecimal code.

```
char copyrightSymbol = '\u00A9';
char omegaSymbol     = '\u03A9';
char newLine         = '\u000A';
```

An implicit conversion from a **char** to a numeric type works for the numeric types that can accommodate an unsigned **short**. For other numeric types, an explicit conversion is required.

String Type

C#'s string type (aliasing the **System.String** type) represents an immutable sequence of Unicode characters. A string literal is specified inside double quotes:

```
string a = "Heat";
```

NOTE

string is a reference type, rather than a value type. Its equality operators, however, follow value-type semantics:

```
string a = "test", b = "test";
Console.Write (a == b);  // True
```

The escape sequences that are valid for **char** literals also work inside strings:

```
string a = "Here's a tab:\t";
```

The cost of this is that whenever you need a literal backslash, you must write it twice:

```
string a1 = "\\\\server\\fileshare\\helloworld.cs";
```

To avoid this problem, C# allows *verbatim* string literals. A verbatim string literal is prefixed with @ and does not support escape sequences. The following verbatim string is identical to the preceding one:

```
string a2 = @"\\server\fileshare\helloworld.cs";
```

A verbatim string literal can also span multiple lines. You can include the double quote character in a verbatim literal by writing it twice.

String concatenation

The + operator concatenates two strings:

```
string s = "a" + "b";
```

The righthand operand may be a non-string value, in which case `ToString` is called on that value. For example:

```
string s = "a" + 5;   // a5
```

Since `string` is immutable, using the + operator repeatedly to build up a string can be inefficient. The solution is to instead use the `System.Text.StringBuilder` type—this represents a mutable (editable) string, and has methods to efficiently `Append`, `Insert`, `Remove` and `Replace` substrings.

String comparisons

`string` does not support < and > operators for comparisons. You must instead use `string`'s `CompareTo` method, which returns a positive number, a negative number, or zero, depending on whether the first value comes after, before, or alongside the second value:

```
Console.Write ("Boston".CompareTo ("Austin"));   // 1
Console.Write ("Boston".CompareTo ("Boston"));   // 0
Console.Write ("Boston".CompareTo ("Chicago"));  // -1
```

Searching within strings

`string`'s indexer returns a character at a specified position:

```
Console.Write ("word"[2]);   // r
```

The `IndexOf`/`LastIndexOf` methods search for a character within the string; the `Contains`, `StartsWith` and `EndsWith` methods search for a substring within the string.

Manipulating strings

Because `string` is immutable, all the methods that "manipulate" a string return a new one, leaving the original untouched:

- Substring extracts a portion of a string.
- Insert and Remove insert and remove characters at a specified position.
- PadLeft and PadRight add whitespace.
- TrimStart, TrimEnd, and Trim remove whitespace.

The string class also defines ToUpper and ToLower methods for changing case, a Split method to split a string into substrings (based on supplied delimiters), and a static Join method to join substrings back into a string.

Arrays

An array represents a fixed number of elements of a particular type. The elements in an array are always stored in a contiguous block of memory, providing highly efficient access.

An array is denoted with square brackets after the element type. The following declares an array of 5 characters:

```
char[] vowels = new char[5];
```

Square brackets also *index* the array, accessing a particular element by position:

```
vowels[0] = 'a'; vowels[1] = 'e'; vowels[2] = 'i';
vowels[3] = 'o'; vowels[4] = 'u';

Console.WriteLine (vowels [1]);      // e
```

This prints "e" because array indexes start at 0. We can use a for loop statement to iterate through each element in the array. The for loop in this example cycles the integer i from 0 to 4:

```
for (int i = 0; i < vowels.Length; i++)
  Console.Write (vowels [i]);            // aeiou
```

Arrays also implement IEnumerable<T> (see "Enumeration and Iterators" on page 125), so you can also enumerate members with the foreach statement:

```
foreach (char c in vowels) Console.Write (c);  // aeiou
```

All array indexing is bounds-checked by the runtime. An `Index OutOfRangeException` is thrown if you use an invalid index:

```
vowels[5] = 'y';   // Runtime error
```

The `Length` property of an array returns the number of elements in the array. Once an array has been created, its length cannot be changed. The `System.Collection` namespace and subnamespaces provide higher-level data structures, such as dynamically sized arrays and dictionaries.

An *array initialization expression* lets you declare and populate an array in a single step:

```
char[] vowels = new char[] {'a','e','i','o','u'};
```

or simply:

```
char[] vowels = {'a','e','i','o','u'};
```

All arrays inherit from the `System.Array` class, which defines common methods and properties for all arrays. This includes instance properties such as `Length` and `Rank`, and static methods to:

- Dynamically create an array (`CreateInstance`)
- Get and set elements regardless of the array type (`Get Value`/`SetValue`)
- Search a sorted array (`BinarySearch`) or an unsorted array (`IndexOf`, `LastIndexOf`, `Find`, `FindIndex`, `FindLastIndex`)
- Sort an array (`Sort`)
- Copy an array (`Copy`)

Default Element Initialization

Creating an array always pre-initializes the elements with default values. The default value for a type is the result of a bitwise zeroing of memory. For example, consider creating an array of integers. Since `int` is a value type, this allocates 1,000 integers in one contiguous block of memory. The default value for each element will be 0:

```
int[] a = new int[1000];
Console.Write (a[123]);              // 0
```

With reference-type elements, the default value is **null**.

An array *itself* is always a reference type object, regardless of element type. For instance, the following is legal:

```
int[] a = null;
```

Multidimensional Arrays

Multidimensional arrays come in two varieties: *rectangular* and *jagged*. Rectangular arrays represent an *n*-dimensional block of memory, and jagged arrays are arrays of arrays.

Rectangular arrays

Rectangular arrays are declared using commas to separate each dimension. The following declares a rectangular two-dimensional array, where the dimensions are 3 × 3:

```
int[,] matrix = new int [3, 3];
```

The GetLength method of an array returns the length for a given dimension (starting at 0):

```
for (int i = 0; i < matrix.GetLength(0); i++)
  for (int j = 0; j < matrix.GetLength(1); j++)
    matrix [i, j] = i * 3 + j;
```

A rectangular array can be initialized as follows (each element in this example is initialized to be identical to the previous example):

```
int[,] matrix = new int[,]
{
  {0,1,2},
  {3,4,5},
  {6,7,8}
};
```

(The code shown in boldface can be omitted in declaration statements such as the one above.)

Jagged arrays

Jagged arrays are declared using successive square brackets to represent each dimension. Here is an example of declaring a jagged two-dimensional array, where the outermost dimension is 3:

```
int[][] matrix = new int[3][];
```

The inner dimensions aren't specified in the declaration. Unlike a rectangular array, each inner array can be an arbitrary length. Each inner array is implicitly initialized to null rather than an empty array. Each inner array must be created manually:

```
for (int i = 0; i < matrix.Length; i++)
{
  matrix[i] = new int [3];        // Create inner array
  for (int j = 0; j < matrix[i].Length; j++)
    matrix[i][j] = i * 3 + j;
}
```

A jagged array can be initialized as follows (each element in this example is initialized to be identical to the previous example):

```
int[][] matrix = new int[][]
{
  new int[] {0,1,2},
  new int[] {3,4,5},
  new int[] {6,7,8}
};
```

(The code shown in boldface can be omitted in declaration statements such as the above.)

Simplified Array Initialization Expressions

We've already seen how to simplify array initialization expressions by omitting the new keyword and type declaration:

```
char[] vowels = new char[] {'a','e','i','o','u'};
char[] vowels =            {'a','e','i','o','u'};
```

Another approach is to omit the type name after the new keyword, and have the compiler *infer* the array type. This is a useful shortcut when passing arrays as arguments. For example, consider the following method:

```
void Foo (char[] data) { ... }
```

We can call this method with an array that we create on the fly, as follows:

```
Foo ( new char[] {'a','e','i','o','u'} );   // Longhand
Foo ( new[]      {'a','e','i','o','u'} );   // Shortcut
```

This shortcut is essential in creating arrays of *anonymous types*, as we'll see later.

Variables and Parameters

A variable represents a storage location that has a modifiable value. A variable can be a *local variable*, *parameter* (*value*, *ref*, or *out*), *field* (*instance* or *static*), or *array element*.

The Stack and the Heap

The stack and the heap are the places where variables and constants reside. Each has very different lifetime semantics.

Stack

The stack is a block of memory for storing local variables and parameters. The stack logically grows and shrinks as a function is entered and exited. Consider the following method (to avoid distraction, input argument checking is ignored):

```
static int Factorial (int x)
{
  if (x == 0) return 1;
  return x * Factorial (x-1);
}
```

This method is recursive, meaning that it calls itself. Each time the method is entered, a new int is allocated on the stack, and each time the method exits, the int is deallocated.

Heap

The heap is a block of memory in which *objects* (i.e., reference-type instances) reside. Whenever a new object is created, it is allocated on the heap, and a reference to that object is returned. During a program's execution, the heap starts filling up as new objects are created. The runtime has a garbage collector that periodically deallocates objects from the heap, so your computer does not run out of memory. An object is eligible for deallocation as soon as nothing references it.

Value-type instances (and object references) live wherever the variable was declared. If the instance was declared as a field within an object, or as an array element, that instance lives on the heap.

NOTE

You can't explicitly delete objects in C#, as you can in C++. An unreferenced object is eventually collected by the garbage collector.

The heap also stores static fields and constants. Unlike objects allocated on the heap (which can get garbage-collected), these live until the application domain is torn down.

Definite Assignment

C# enforces a definite assignment policy. In practice, this means that outside of an **unsafe** context, it's impossible to access uninitialized memory. Definite assignment has three implications:

- Local variables must be assigned a value before they can be read.
- Function arguments must be supplied when a method is called (unless marked optional—see "Optional parameters (C# 4.0)" on page 40).

- All other variables (such as fields and array elements) are automatically initialized by the runtime.

For example, the following code results in a compile-time error:

```
static void Main()
{
  int x;
  Console.WriteLine (x);        // Compile-time error
}
```

However, if x were instead a *field* of the containing class, this would be legal and would print 0.

Default Values

All type instances have a default value. The default value for the predefined types is the result of a bitwise zeroing of memory, and is null for reference types, 0 for numeric and enum types, '\0' for the char type, and false for the bool type.

You can obtain the default value for any type using the default keyword (in practice, this is useful with generics, as we'll see later). The default value in a custom value type (i.e., struct) is the same as the default value for each field defined by the custom type.

Parameters

A method has a sequence of parameters. Parameters define the set of arguments that must be provided for that method. In this example, the method Foo has a single parameter named p, of type int:

```
static void Foo (int p)    // p is a parameter
{
  ...
}
static void Main() { Foo (8); }    // 8 is an argument
```

You can control how parameters are passed with the `ref` and `out` modifiers:

Parameter modifier	Passed by	Variable must be definitely assigned
None	Value	Going *in*
Ref	Reference	Going *in*
out	Reference	Going *out*

Passing arguments by value

By default, arguments in C# are *passed by value*, which is by far the most common case. This means a copy of the value is created when passed to the method:

```
static void Foo (int p)
{
  p = p + 1;              // Increment p by 1
  Console.WriteLine (p);  // Write p to screen
}
static void Main()
{
  int x = 8;
  Foo (x);                // Make a copy of x
  Console.WriteLine (x);  // x will still be 8
}
```

Assigning `p` a new value does not change the contents of `x`, since `p` and `x` reside in different memory locations.

Passing a reference-type argument by value copies the *reference*, but not the object. In the following example, `Foo` sees the same `StringBuilder` object that `Main` instantiated, but has an independent *reference* to it. In other words, `sb` and `fooSB` are separate variables that reference the same `StringBuilder` object:

```
static void Foo (StringBuilder fooSB)
{
  fooSB.Append ("test");
  fooSB = null;
}
static void Main()
{
```

```
      StringBuilder sb = new StringBuilder();
      Foo (sb);
      Console.WriteLine (sb.ToString());    // test
    }
```

Because fooSB is a *copy* of a reference, setting it to null doesn't make sb null. (If, however, fooSB was declared and called with the ref modifier, sb *would* become null.)

The ref modifier

To *pass by reference*, C# provides the ref parameter modifier. In the following example, p and x refer to the same memory locations:

```
    static void Foo (ref int p)
    {
      p = p + 1;
      Console.WriteLine (p);
    }
    static void Main()
    {
      int x = 8;
      Foo (ref x);              // Pass x by reference
      Console.WriteLine (x);    // x is now 9
    }
```

Now assigning p a new value changes the contents of x. Notice how the ref modifier is required both when writing and when calling the method. This makes it very clear what's going on.

NOTE

A parameter can be passed by reference or by value, regardless of whether the parameter type is a reference type or a value type.

The out modifier

An out argument is like a ref argument, except it:

- Need not be assigned before going into the function
- Must be assigned before it comes *out* of the function

The **out** modifier is most commonly used to get multiple return values back from a method.

The params modifier

The `params` parameter modifier may be specified on the last parameter of a method so that the method accepts any number of parameters of a particular type. The parameter type must be declared as an array. For example:

```
static int Sum (params int[] ints)
{
  int sum = 0;
  for (int i = 0; i < ints.Length; i++) sum += ints[i];
  return sum;
}
```

We can call this as follows:

```
Console.WriteLine (Sum (1, 2, 3, 4));    // 10
```

You can also supply a `params` argument as an ordinary array. The preceding call is semantically equivalent to:

```
Console.WriteLine (new int[] { 1, 2, 3, 4 } );
```

Optional parameters (C# 4.0)

From C# 4.0, methods, constructors, and indexers can declare *optional parameters*. A parameter is optional if it specifies a *default value* in its declaration:

```
void Foo (int x = 23) { Console.WriteLine (x); }
```

Optional parameters may be omitted when calling the method:

```
Foo();      // 23
```

The *default argument* of 23 is actually *passed* to the optional parameter x—the compiler bakes the value 23 into the compiled code at the *calling* side. The preceding call to Foo is semantically identical to:

```
Foo (23);
```

because the compiler simply substitutes the default value of an optional parameter wherever it is used.

The default value of an optional parameter must be specified by a constant expression, or a parameterless constructor of a value type. Optional parameters cannot be marked with **ref** or **out**.

Mandatory parameters must occur *before* optional parameters in both the method declaration and method call (the exception is with **params** arguments, which still always come last). In the following example, the explicit value of **1** is passed to **x**, and the default value of **0** is passed to **y**:

```
void Foo (int x = 0, int y = 0)
{
  Console.WriteLine (x + ", " + y);
}
void Test()
{
  Foo(1);    // 1, 0
}
```

To do the converse (pass a default value to **x** and an explicit value to **y**) you must combine optional parameters with *named arguments*.

Named arguments (C# 4.0)

Rather than identifying an argument by position, you can identify an argument by name. For example:

```
void Foo (int x, int y)
{
  Console.WriteLine (x + ", " + y);
}
void Test()
{
```

```
    Foo (x:1, y:2);  // 1, 2
}
```

Named arguments can occur in any order. The following calls
to Foo are semantically identical:

```
Foo (x:1, y:2);
Foo (y:2, x:1);
```

You can mix named and positional parameters, as long as the
named arguments appear last:

```
Foo (1, y:2);
```

Named arguments are particularly useful in conjunction with
optional parameters. For instance, consider the following
method:

```
void Bar (int a=0, int b=0, int c=0, int d=0) { ... }
```

We can call this by supplying only a value for d as follows:

```
Bar (d:3);
```

This is particularly useful when calling COM APIs.

var—Implicitly Typed Local Variables

It is often the case that you declare and initialize a variable in
one step. If the compiler is able to infer the type from the initialization expression, you can use the word var in place of the
type declaration. For example:

```
var x = "hello";
var y = new System.Text.StringBuilder();
var z = (float)Math.PI;
```

This is precisely equivalent to:

```
string x = "hello";
System.Text.StringBuilder y =
  new System.Text.StringBuilder();
float z = (float)Math.PI;
```

Because of this direct equivalence, implicitly typed variables
are statically typed. For example, the following generates a
compile-time error:

```
var x = 5;
x = "hello";      // Compile-time error; x is of type int
```

In the section "Anonymous Types" on page 140, we describe a scenario where the use of **var** is mandatory.

Expressions and Operators

An *expression* essentially denotes a value. The simplest kinds of expressions are constants (such as **123**) and variables (such as **x**). Expressions can be transformed and combined using operators. An *operator* takes one or more input *operands* to output a new expression:

```
12 * 30    // * is an operator; 12 and 30 are operands.
```

Complex expressions can be built because an operand may itself be an expression, such as the operand (**12** * **30**) in the following example:

```
1 + (12 * 30)
```

Operators in C# are classed as *unary*, *binary*, or *ternary*—depending on the number of operands they work on (one, two, or three). The binary operators always use *infix* notation, where the operator is placed *between* the two operands.

Operators that are intrinsic to the basic plumbing of the language are called *primary*; an example is the method call operator. An expression that has no value is called a *void expression*:

```
Console.WriteLine (1)
```

Since a void expression has no value, it cannot be used as an operand to build more complex expressions:

```
1 + Console.WriteLine (1)      // Compile-time error
```

Assignment Expressions

An assignment expression uses the = operator to assign the result of another expression to a variable. For example:

```
x = x * 5
```

An assignment expression is not a void expression. It actually carries the assignment value, and so can be incorporated into another expression. In the following example, the expression assigns 2 to x and 10 to y:

```
y = 5 * (x = 2)
```

This style of expression can be used to initialize multiple values:

```
a = b = c = d = 0
```

The *compound assignment operators* are syntactic shortcuts that combine assignment with another operator. For example:

```
x *= 2     // equivalent to x = x * 2
x <<= 1    // equivalent to x = x << 1
```

(A subtle exception to this rule is with *events*, described further in "Event Accessors" on page 111: the += and -= operators here are treated specially, and map to the event's add and remove accessors).

Operator Precedence and Associativity

When an expression contains multiple operators, *precedence* and *associativity* determine the order of evaluation. Operators with higher precedence execute before operators of lower precedence. If the operators have the same precedence, the operator's associativity determines the order of evaluation.

Precedence

The expression 1 + 2 * 3 is evaluated as 1 + (2 * 3) because * has a higher precedence than +.

Left-associative operators

Binary operators (except for assignment, lambda, and null coalescing operators) are *left-associative*; in other words, they are evaluated from left to right. For example, the expression 8/4/2 is evaluated as (8/4)/2 due to left associativity. Of course, you can insert your own parentheses to change evaluation order.

Right-associative operators

The *assignment operators*, lambda, null coalescing and conditional operator are *right-associative*; in other words, they are evaluated from right to left. Right associativity allows multiple assignments such as x=y=3 to compile: it works by first assigning 3 to y, and then assigning the result of that expression (3) to x.

Operator Table

The following table lists C#'s operators in order of precedence. Operators listed under the same subheading have the same precedence. We explain user-overloadable operators in the section "Operator Overloading" on page 135.

Operator symbol	Operator name	Example	Overloadable
Primary (highest precedence)			
( )	Grouping	while(x)	No
.	Member access	x.y	No
->	Pointer to struct (unsafe)	x->y	No
( )	Function call	x( )	No
[ ]	Array/index	a[x]	Via indexer
++	Post-increment	x++	Yes
--	Post-decrement	x--	Yes
new	Create instance	new Foo( )	No
stackalloc	Unsafe stack allocation	stackalloc(10)	No
typeof	Get type from identifier	typeof(int)	No
checked	Integral overflow check on	checked(x)	No
unchecked	Integral overflow check off	unchecked(x)	No

Unary			
sizeof	Get size of struct	sizeof(int)	No
+	Positive value of	+x	Yes
-	Negative value of	-x	Yes
!	Not	!x	Yes
~	Bitwise complement	~x	Yes
++	Pre-increment	++x	Yes
--	Pre-decrement	--x	Yes
()	Cast	(int)x	No
*	Value at address (unsafe)	*x	No
&	Address of value (unsafe)	&x	No

Multiplicative			
*	Multiply	x * y	Yes
/	Divide	x / y	Yes
%	Remainder	x % y	Yes

Additive			
+	Add	x + y	Yes
-	Subtract	x - y	Yes

Shift			
<<	Shift left	x >> 1	Yes
>>	Shift right	x << 1	Yes

Relational			
<	Less than	x < y	Yes
>	Greater than	x > y	Yes
<=	Less than or equal to	x <= y	Yes
>=	Greater than or equal to	x >= y	Yes
is	Type is or is subclass of	x is y	No

Relational			
as	Type conversion	x as y	No
Equality			
==	Equals	x == y	Yes
!=	Not equals	x != y	Yes
Logical And			
&	And	x & y	Yes
Logical Xor			
^	Exclusive Or	x ^ y	Yes
Logical Or			
|	Or	x | y	Yes
Conditional And			
&&	Conditional And	x && y	Via &
Conditional Or			
||	Conditional Or	x || y	Via |
Conditional			
? :	Conditional	isTrue ? thenThis : elseThis	No
Assignment			
=	Assign	x = y	No
*=	Multiply self by	x *= 2	Via *
/=	Divide self by	x /= 2	Via /
+=	Add to self	x += 2	Via +
-=	Subtract from self	x -= 2	Via -
<<=	Shift self left by	x <<= 2	Via <<
>>=	Shift self right by	x >>= 2	Via >>
&=	And self by	x &= 2	Via &
^=	Exclusive-Or self by	x ^= 2	Via ^
|=	Or self by	x |= 2	Via |

Lambda (lowest precedence)			
=>	Lambda	x => x + 1	No

Statements

Functions comprise statements that execute sequentially in the textual order in which they appear. A *statement block* is a series of statements appearing between braces (the {} tokens).

Declaration Statements

A declaration statement declares a new variable, optionally initializing the variable with an expression. A declaration statement ends in a semicolon. You may declare multiple variables of the same type in a comma-separated list. For example:

```
bool rich = true, famous = false;
```

A constant declaration is like a variable declaration, except that the variable cannot be changed after it has been declared, and the initialization must occur with the declaration:

```
const double c = 2.99792458E08;
```

Local variable scope

The scope of a local or constant variable extends throughout the current block. You cannot declare another local variable with the same name in the current block or in any nested blocks.

Expression Statements

Expression statements are expressions that are also valid statements. In practice, this means expressions that "do" something; in other words, expressions that:

- Assign or modify a variable
- Instantiate an object
- Call a method

Expressions that do none of these are not valid statements:

```
string s = "foo";
s.Length;              // Illegal statement: does nothing!
```

When you call a constructor or a method that returns a value, you're not obliged to use the result. However, unless the constructor or method changes state, the statement is useless:

```
new StringBuilder();     // Legal, but useless
x.Equals (y);            // Legal, but useless
```

Selection Statements

Selection statements conditionally control the flow of program execution.

The if statement

An if statement executes a body of code depending on whether a bool expression is true. For example:

```
if (5 < 2 * 3)
{
  Console.WriteLine ("true");     // True
}
```

If the body of code is a single statement, you can optionally omit the braces:

```
if (5 < 2 * 3)
  Console.WriteLine ("true");     // True
```

The else clause

An if statement is optionally followed by an else clause:

```
if (2 + 2 == 5)
  Console.WriteLine ("Does not compute");
else
  Console.WriteLine ("False");    // False
```

Within an else clause, you can nest another if statement:

```
if (2 + 2 == 5)
  Console.WriteLine ("Does not compute");
```

```
else
  if (2 + 2 == 4)
    Console.WriteLine ("Computes");        // Computes
```

Changing the flow of execution with braces

An else clause always applies to the immediately preceding
if statement in the statement block. For example:

```
if (true)
  if (false)
    Console.WriteLine();
  else
    Console.WriteLine ("executes");
```

This is semantically identical to:

```
if (true)
{
  if (false)
    Console.WriteLine();
  else
    Console.WriteLine ("executes");
}
```

We can change the execution flow by moving the braces:

```
if (true)
{
  if (false)
    Console.WriteLine();
}
else
  Console.WriteLine ("does not execute");
```

C# has no "elseif" keyword; however, the following pattern
achieves the same result:

```
static void TellMeWhatICanDo (int age)
{
  if (age >= 35)
    Console.WriteLine ("You can be president!");
  else if (age >= 21)
    Console.WriteLine ("You can drink!");
  else if (age >= 18)
    Console.WriteLine ("You can vote!");
  else
    Console.WriteLine ("You can wait!");
}
```

The switch statement

switch statements let you branch program execution based on a selection of possible values that a variable may have. switch statements may result in cleaner code than multiple if statements, since switch statements only require an expression to be evaluated once. For instance:

```
static void ShowCard (int cardNumber)
{
  switch (cardNumber)
  {
    case 13:
      Console.WriteLine ("King");
      break;
    case 12:
      Console.WriteLine ("Queen");
      break;
    case 11:
      Console.WriteLine ("Jack");
      break;
    default:      // Any other cardNumber
      Console.WriteLine (cardNumber);
      break;
  }
}
```

You can only switch on an expression of a type that can be statically evaluated, which restricts it to the built-in integral types, string type, and enum types. At the end of each case clause, you must say explicitly where execution is to go next, with some kind of jump statement. Here are the options:

- break (jumps to the end of the switch statement)
- goto case x (jumps to another case clause)
- goto default (jumps to the default clause)
- Any other jump statement—namely, return, throw, continue, or goto label

When more than one value should execute the same code, you can list the common cases sequentially:

```
switch (cardNumber)
{
  case 13:
  case 12:
  case 11:
    Console.WriteLine ("Face card");
    break;
  default:
    Console.WriteLine ("Plain card");
    break;
}
```

This feature of a switch statement can be pivotal in terms of producing cleaner code than multiple if-else statements.

Iteration Statements

C# enables a sequence of statements to execute repeatedly with the while, do-while, for and foreach statements.

while and do-while loops

while loops repeatedly execute a body of code while a bool expression is true. The expression is tested *before* the body of the loop is executed. For example, the following writes 012:

```
int i = 0;
while (i < 3)
{                          // Braces here are optional
  Console.Write (i++);
}
```

do-while loops differ in functionality from while loops, only in that they test the expression *after* the statement block has executed (ensuring that the block is always executed at least once). Here's the preceding example rewritten with a do-while loop:

```
int i = 0;
do
{
  Console.WriteLine (i++);
}
while (i < 3);
```

for loops

for loops are like while loops with special clauses for *initialization* and *iteration* of a loop variable. A for loop contains three clauses as follows:

```
for (init-clause; condition-clause; iteration-clause)
  statement-or-statement-block
```

The *init-clause* executes before the loop begins, and typically initializes one or more *iteration* variables.

The *condition-clause* is a bool expression which is tested *before* each loop iteration. The body executes while this condition is true.

The *iteration-clause* is executed *after* each iteration of the body. It's typically used to update the iteration variable.

For example, the following prints the numbers 0 through 2:

```
for (int i = 0; i < 3; i++)
  Console.WriteLine (i);
```

The following prints the first 10 Fibonacci numbers (where each number is the sum of the previous two):

```
for (int i = 0, prevFib = 1, curFib = 1; i < 10; i++)
{
  Console.WriteLine (prevFib);
  int newFib = prevFib + curFib;
  prevFib = curFib; curFib = newFib;
}
```

Any of the three parts of the for statement may be omitted. One can implement an infinite loop such as the following (though while(true) may be used instead):

```
for (;;) Console.WriteLine ("interrupt me");
```

foreach loops

The foreach statement iterates over each element in an enumerable object. Most of the types in C# and the .NET Framework that represent a set or list of elements are enumerable. For example, both an array and a string are enumerable. Here is an example of enumerating over the characters in a string, from the first character to the last:

```
foreach (char c in "beer")
  Console.WriteLine (c + " ");   // b e e r
```

We define enumerable objects in "Enumeration and Iterators" on page 125.

Jump Statements

The C# jump statements are break, continue, goto, return, and throw. We cover the throw keyword in "try Statements and Exceptions" on page 117.

The break statement

The break statement ends the execution of the body of an iteration or switch statement:

```
int x = 0;
while (true)
{
  if (x++ > 5) break;      // break from the loop
}
// execution continues here after break
...
```

The continue statement

The continue statement forgoes the remaining statements in the loop and makes an early start on the next iteration. The following loop *skips* even numbers:

```
for (int i = 0; i < 10; i++)
{
  if ((i % 2) == 0) continue;
  Console.Write (i + " ");     // 1 3 5 7 9
}
```

The goto statement

The goto statement transfers execution to a label (denoted with a colon suffix) within a statement block. The following iterates the numbers 1 through 5, mimicking a **for** loop:

```
int i = 1;
startLoop:
if (i <= 5)
{
  Console.Write (i + " ");   // 1 2 3 4 5
  i++;
  goto startLoop;
}
```

The return statement

The return statement exits the method and must return an expression of the method's return type if the method is nonvoid:

```
static decimal AsPercentage (decimal d)
{
  decimal p = d * 100m;
  return p;      // Return to calling method with value
}
```

A return statement can appear anywhere in a method.

Namespaces

A namespace is a domain within which type names must be unique. Types are typically organized into hierarchical namespaces—both to avoid naming conflicts and to make type names easier to find. For example, the RSA type that handles public key encryption is defined within the following namespace:

```
System.Security.Cryptography
```

A namespace forms an integral part of a type's name. The following code calls RSA's **Create** method:

```
System.Security.Cryptography.RSA rsa =
  System.Security.Cryptography.RSA.Create();
```

The **namepace** keyword defines a namespace for types within that block. For example:

```
namespace Outer.Middle.Inner
{
  class Class1 {}
  class Class2 {}
}
```

The dots in the namespace indicate a hierarchy of nested namespaces. The code that follows is semantically identical to the preceding example.

```
namespace Outer
{
  namespace Middle
  {
    namespace Inner
    {
      class Class1 {}
      class Class2 {}
    }
  }
}
```

You can refer to a type with its *fully qualified name*, which includes all namespaces from the outermost to the innermost. For example, we could refer to `Class1` in the preceding example as `Outer.Middle.Inner.Class1`.

Types not defined in any namespace are said to reside in the *global namespace*. The global namespace also includes top-level namespaces, such as `Outer` in our example.

The using Directive

The using directive *imports* a namespace and is a convenient way to refer to types without their fully qualified names. For example, we can refer to Class1 in the preceding example as follows:

```
using Outer.Middle.Inner;

class Test     // Test is in the global namespace
{
  static void Main()
  {
    Class1 c;    // Don't need fully qualified name
    ...
  }
}
```

A using directive can be nested within a namespace itself, to limit the scope of the directive.

Rules Within a Namespace

Name scoping

Names declared in outer namespaces can be used unqualified within inner namespaces. In this example, the names Middle and Class1 are implicitly imported into Inner:

```
namespace Outer
{
  namespace Middle
  {
    class Class1 {}

    namespace Inner
    {
      class Class2 : Class1 {}
    }
  }
}
```

If you want to refer to a type in a different branch of your namespace hierarchy, you can use a partially qualified name.

As you can see in the following example, we base Sales Report on Common.ReportBase:

```
namespace MyTradingCompany
{
  namespace Common
  {
    class ReportBase {}
  }
  namespace ManagementReporting
  {
    class SalesReport : Common.ReportBase {}
  }
}
```

Name hiding

If the same type name appears in both an inner and outer namespace, the inner name wins. To refer to the type in the outer namespace, you must qualify its name.

NOTE

All type names are converted to fully qualified names at compile time. Intermediate Language (IL) code contains no unqualified or partially qualified names.

Repeated namespaces

You can repeat a namespace declaration, as long as the type names within the namespaces don't conflict:

```
namespace Outer.Middle.Inner { class Class1 {} }
namespace Outer.Middle.Inner { class Class2 {} }
```

The classes can even span source files and assemblies.

The global:: qualifier

Occasionally, a fully qualified type name may conflict with an inner name. You can force C# to use the fully qualified type name by prefixing it with global:: as follows:

```
global::System.Text.StringBuilder sb;
```

Aliasing Types and Namespaces

Importing a namespace can result in type-name collision. Rather than importing the whole namespace, you can import just the specific types you need, giving each type an alias. For example:

```
using PropertyInfo2 = System.Reflection.PropertyInfo;
class Program { PropertyInfo2 p; }
```

An entire namespace can be aliased, as follows:

```
using R = System.Reflection;
class Program { R.PropertyInfo p; }
```

Classes

A class is the most common kind of reference type. The simplest possible class declaration is as follows:

```
class Foo
{
}
```

Optionally, a more complex class has the following:

Preceding the keyword class	*Attributes* and *class modifiers*. The non-nested class modifiers are public, internal, abstract, sealed, static, unsafe, and partial.
Following YourClassName	*Generic type parameters*, a *base class*, and *interfaces*.
Within the braces	*Class members* (these are *methods*, *properties*, *indexers*, *events*, *fields*, *constructors*, *operator functions*, *nested types*, and a *finalizer*).

Fields

A *field* is a variable that is a member of a class or struct. For example:

```
class Octopus
{
  string name;
```

```
    public int Age = 10;
}
```

A field may have the **readonly** modifier to prevent it from being modified after construction. A read-only field can be assigned only in its declaration or within the enclosing type's constructor.

Field initialization is optional. An uninitialized field has a default value (0, \0, **null**, **false**). Field initializers run before constructors, in the order in which they appear.

For convenience, you may declare multiple fields of the same type in a comma-separated list. This is a convenient way for all the fields to share the same attributes and field modifiers. For example:

```
static readonly int legs = 8, eyes = 1;
```

Methods

A method performs an action in a series of statements. A method can receive *input* data from the caller by specifying *parameters* and *output* data back to the caller by specifying a *return type*. A method can specify a **void** return type, indicating that it doesn't return any value to its caller. A method can also output data back to the caller via **ref**/**out** parameters.

A method's *signature* must be unique within the type. A method's signature comprises its name and parameter types (but not the parameter *names*, nor the return type).

Overloading methods

A type may overload methods (have multiple methods with the same name), as long as the parameter types are different. For example, the following methods can all coexist in the same type:

```
void Foo (int x);
void Foo (double x);
void Foo (int x, float y);
void Foo (float x, int y);
```

Instance Constructors

Constructors run initialization code on a class or struct. A constructor is defined like a method, except the method name and return type are reduced to the name of the enclosing type:

```
public class Panda
{
  string name;              // Define field
  public Panda (string n)   // Define constructor
  {
    name = n;               // Initialization code
  }
}
...
Panda p = new Panda ("Petey");   // Call constructor
```

A class or struct may overload constructors. One overload may call another, using the **this** keyword:

```
public class Wine
{
  public Wine (decimal price) {...}

  public Wine (decimal price, int year)
               : this (price) {...}
}
```

When one constructor calls another, the *called constructor* executes first.

You can pass an *expression* into another constructor as follows:

```
public Wine (decimal price, DateTime year)
             : this (price, year.Year) {...}
```

The expression itself cannot make use of the **this** reference, for example, to call an instance method. It can, however, call static methods.

Implicit parameterless constructors

For classes, the C# compiler automatically generates a parameterless constructor if and only if you do not define any constructors. However, as soon as you define at least one constructor, the parameterless constructor is no longer automatically generated.

For structs, a parameterless constructor is intrinsic to the struct; therefore, you cannot define your own. The role of a struct's implicit parameterless constructor is to initialize each field with default values.

Nonpublic constructors

Constructors do not need to be public. A common reason to have a nonpublic constructor is to control instance creation via a static method call. The static method could be used to return an object from a pool rather than creating a new object, or return a specialized subclass chosen based on input arguments.

Object Initializers

To simplify object initialization, the accessible fields or properties of an object can be initialized in a single statement directly after construction. For example, consider the following class:

```
public class Bunny
{
  public string Name;
  public bool LikesCarrots, LikesHumans;

  public Bunny () {}
  public Bunny (string n) { Name = n; }
}
```

Using object initializers, you can instantiate **Bunny** objects as follows:

```
Bunny b1 = new Bunny {
                       Name="Bo",
                       LikesCarrots = true,
                       LikesHumans = false
                     };
```

```
Bunny b2 = new Bunny ("Bo") {
                            LikesCarrots = true,
                            LikesHumans = false
                        };
```

The this Reference

The this reference refers to the instance itself. In the following
example, the Marry method uses this to set the partner's
mate field:

```
public class Panda
{
  public Panda Mate;

  public void Marry (Panda partner)
  {
    Mate = partner;
    partner.Mate = this;
  }
}
```

The this reference also disambiguates a local variable or parameter from a field. For example:

```
public class Test
{
  string name;
  public Test (string name) { this.name = name; }
}
```

The this reference is valid only within nonstatic members of a
class or struct.

Properties

Properties look like fields from the outside, but internally they
contain logic, like methods do. For example, you can't tell by
looking at the following code whether CurrentPrice is a field
or a property:

```
Stock msft = new Stock();
msft.CurrentPrice = 30;
msft.CurrentPrice -= 3;
Console.WriteLine (msft.CurrentPrice);
```

A property is declared like a field, but with a `get`/`set` block added. Here's how to implement `CurrentPrice` as a property:

```
public class Stock
{
  decimal currentPrice;  // The private "backing" field

  public decimal CurrentPrice   // The public property
  {
    get { return currentPrice; }
    set { currentPrice = value; }
  }
}
```

`get` and `set` denote property *accessors*. The `get` accessor runs when the property is read. It must return a value of the property's type. The `set` accessor runs when the property is assigned. It has an implicit parameter named `value` of the property's type that you typically assign to a private field (in this case, `currentPrice`).

Although properties are accessed in the same way as fields, they differ in that they give the implementer complete control over getting and setting its value. This control enables the implementer to choose whatever internal representation is needed, without exposing the internal details to the user of the property. In this example, the `set` method could throw an exception if `value` was outside a valid range of values.

NOTE

Throughout this book, we use public fields to keep the examples free of distraction. In a real application, you would typically favor public properties over public fields to promote encapsulation.

A property is read-only if it specifies only a `get` accessor, and it is write-only if it specifies only a `set` accessor. Write-only properties are rarely used. A property typically has a dedicated backing field to store the underlying data. However, it need not—it may instead return a value computed from other data.

Automatic properties

The most common implementation for a property is a getter and/or setter that simply reads and writes to a private field of the same type as the property. An *automatic property* declaration instructs the compiler to provide this implementation. We can redeclare the first example in this section as follows:

```
public class Stock
{
  public decimal CurrentPrice { get; set; }
}
```

The compiler automatically generates a private backing field of a compiler-generated name that cannot be referred to. The set accessor can be marked **private** if you want to expose the property as read-only to other types.

get and set accessibility

The get and set accessors can have different access levels. The typical use case for this is to have a **public** property with an **internal** or **private** access modifier on the setter:

```
private decimal x;
public decimal X
{
  get        { return x;  }
  private set { x = Math.Round (value, 2); }
}
```

Notice that you declare the property itself with the more permissive access level (**public**, in this case), and add the modifier to the accessor you want to be *less* accessible.

Indexers

Indexers provide a natural syntax for accessing elements in a class or struct that encapsulate a list or dictionary of values. Indexers are similar to properties, but are accessed via an index argument rather than a property name. The **string** class has an indexer that lets you access each of its **char** values via an **int** index:

```
string s = "hello";
Console.WriteLine (s[0]); // 'h'
Console.WriteLine (s[3]); // 'l'
```

The syntax for using indexers is like that for using arrays when the index is an integer type.

Implementing an indexer

To write an indexer, define a property called `this`, specifying the arguments in square brackets. For instance:

```
class Sentence
{
  string[] words = "The quick brown fox".Split();

  public string this [int wordNum]        // indexer
  {
    get { return words [wordNum];  }
    set { words [wordNum] = value; }
  }
}
```

Here's how we could use this indexer:

```
Sentence s = new Sentence();
Console.WriteLine (s[3]);        // fox
s[3] = "kangaroo";
Console.WriteLine (s[3]);        // kangaroo
```

A type may declare multiple indexers, each with parameters of different types. An indexer can also take more than one parameter:

```
public string this [int arg1, string arg2]
{
  get { ... }  set { ... }
}
```

If you omit the `set` accessor, an indexer becomes read-only.

Constants

A *constant* is a field whose value can never change. A constant is evaluated statically at compile time and the compiler literally substitutes its value whenever used, rather like a macro in

---

C++. A constant can be any of the built-in numeric types, `bool`, `char`, `string`, or an enum type.

A constant is declared with the `const` keyword and must be initialized with a value. For example:

```
public class Test
{
  public const string Message = "Hello World";
}
```

A constant is much more restrictive than a `static readonly` field—both in the types you can use and in field initialization semantics. A constant also differs from a `static readonly` field in that the evaluation of the constant occurs at compile time. Constants can also be declared local to a method:

```
static void Main()
{
  const double twoPI = 2 * System.Math.PI;
  ...
}
```

Static Constructors

A static constructor executes once per *type*, rather than once per *instance*. A type can define only one static constructor, and it must be parameterless and have the same name as the type:

```
class Test
{
  static Test() { Console.Write ("Type Initialized"); }
}
```

The runtime automatically invokes a static constructor just prior to the type being used. Two things trigger this: instantiating the type, and accessing a static member in the type.

WARNING

If a static constructor throws an unhandled exception, that type becomes *unusable* for the life of the application.

Static field initializers run just *before* the static constructor is called. If a type has no static constructor, field initializers will execute just prior to the type being used—or *anytime earlier* at the whim of the runtime. (This means that the presence of a static constructor may cause field initializers to execute later in the program than they would otherwise.)

Static Classes

A class can be marked `static`, indicating that it must be composed solely of static members and cannot be subclassed. The `System.Console` and `System.Math` classes are good examples of static classes.

Finalizers

Finalizers are class-only methods that execute before the garbage collector reclaims the memory for an unreferenced object. The syntax for a finalizer is the name of the class prefixed with the ~ symbol:

```
class Class1
{
  ~Class1() { ... }
}
```

C# translates a finalizer into a method that overrides the `Finalize` method in the `object` class. We discuss garbage collection and finalizers fully in Chapter 12 of *C# 4.0 in a Nutshell* (O'Reilly).

Partial Types and Methods

Partial types allow a type definition to be split—typically across multiple files. A common scenario is for a partial class to be auto-generated from some other source (e.g., an XSD), and for that class to be augmented with additional hand-authored methods. For example:

```
// PaymentFormGen.cs - auto-generated
partial class PaymentForm { ... }
```

```
// PaymentForm.cs - hand-authored
partial class PaymentForm { ... }
```

Each participant must have the `partial` declaration.

Participants cannot have conflicting members. A constructor with the same parameters, for instance, cannot be repeated. Partial types are resolved entirely by the compiler, which means that each participant must be available at compile time and must reside in the same assembly.

A base class may be specified on a single participant or on all participants. In addition, each participant can independently specify interfaces to implement. We cover base classes and interfaces in the sections "Inheritance" on page 70 and "Interfaces" on page 85.

Partial methods

A partial type may contain *partial methods*. These let an auto-generated partial type provide customizable hooks for manual authoring. For example:

```
partial class PaymentForm      // In auto-generated file
{
  partial void ValidatePayment (decimal amount);
}

partial class PaymentForm      // In hand-authored file
{
  partial void ValidatePayment (decimal amount)
  {
    if (amount > 100) Console.Write ("Expensive!");
  }
}
```

A partial method consists of two parts: a *definition* and an *implementation*. The definition is typically written by a code generator, and the implementation is typically manually authored. If an implementation is not provided, the definition of the partial method is compiled away. This allows auto-generated code to be liberal in providing hooks, without having to worry about code bloat. Partial methods must be **void** and are implicitly **private**.

Inheritance

A class can *inherit* from another class to extend or customize the original class. Inheriting from a class lets you reuse the functionality in that class instead of building it from scratch. A class can inherit from only a single class, but can itself be inherited by many classes, thus forming a class hierarchy. In this example, we start by defining a class called **Asset**:

```
public class Asset { public string Name; }
```

Next, we define classes called **Stock** and **House**, which will inherit from **Asset**. **Stock** and **House** get everything an **Asset** has, plus any additional members that they define:

```
public class Stock : Asset    // inherits from Asset
{
  public long SharesOwned;
}

public class House : Asset    // inherits from Asset
{
  public decimal Mortgage;
}
```

Here's how we can use these classes:

```
Stock msft = new Stock { Name="MSFT",
                         SharesOwned=1000 };

Console.WriteLine (msft.Name);         // MSFT
Console.WriteLine (msft.SharesOwned);  // 1000

House mansion = new House { Name="Mansion",
                            Mortgage=250000 };

Console.WriteLine (mansion.Name);      // Mansion
Console.WriteLine (mansion.Mortgage);  // 250000
```

The *subclasses*, **Stock** and **House**, inherit the **Name** property from the *base class*, **Asset**.

Subclasses are also called *derived classes*.

Polymorphism

References are polymorphic. This means a variable of type x can refer to an object that subclasses x. For instance, consider the following method:

```
public static void Display (Asset asset)
{
  System.Console.WriteLine (asset.Name);
}
```

This method can display both a `Stock` and a `House`, since they are both `Asset`s. Polymorphism works on the basis that subclasses (`Stock` and `House`) have all the features of their base class (`Asset`). The converse, however, is not true. If `Display` was rewritten to accept a `House`, you could not pass in an `Asset`.

Casting and Reference Conversions

An object reference can be:

- Implicitly *upcast* to a base class reference
- Explicitly *downcast* to a subclass reference

Upcasting and downcasting between compatible reference types performs *reference conversions*: a new reference is created that points to the *same* object. An upcast always succeeds; a downcast succeeds only if the object is suitably typed.

Upcasting

An upcast operation creates a base class reference from a subclass reference. For example:

```
Stock msft = new Stock();    // From previous example
Asset a = msft;              // Upcast
```

After the upcast, variable `a` still references the same `Stock` object as variable `msft`. The object being referenced is not itself altered or converted:

```
Console.WriteLine (a == msft);        // True
```

Although a and msft refer to the identical object, a has a more restrictive view on that object:

```
Console.WriteLine (a.Name);           // OK
Console.WriteLine (a.SharesOwned);    // Error
```

The last line generates a compile-time error because the variable a is of type Asset, even though it refers to an object of type Stock. To get to its SharesOwned field, you must *downcast* the Asset to a Stock.

Downcasting

A downcast operation creates a subclass reference from a base class reference. For example:

```
Stock msft = new Stock();
Asset a = msft;                       // Upcast
Stock s = (Stock)a;                   // Downcast
Console.WriteLine (s.SharesOwned);    // <No error>
Console.WriteLine (s == a);           // True
Console.WriteLine (s == msft);        // True
```

As with an upcast, only references are affected—not the underlying object. A downcast requires an explicit cast because it can potentially fail at runtime:

```
House h = new House();
Asset a = h;            // Upcast always succeeds
Stock s = (Stock)a;     // Downcast fails: a is not a Stock
```

If a downcast fails, an InvalidCastException is thrown. This is an example of *runtime type checking* (see "Static and Runtime Type Checking" on page 80).

The as operator

The as operator performs a downcast that evaluates to null (rather than throwing an exception) if the downcast fails:

```
Asset a = new Asset();
Stock s = a as Stock;   // s is null; no exception thrown
```

This is useful when you're going to subsequently test whether the result is null:

```
if (s != null) Console.WriteLine (s.SharesOwned);
```

The as operator cannot perform *custom conversions* (see "Operator Overloading" on page 135) and it cannot do numeric conversions.

The is operator

The is operator tests whether a reference conversion would succeed; in other words, whether an object derives from a specified class (or implements an interface). It is often used to test before downcasting:

```
if (a is Stock) Console.Write (((Stock)a).SharesOwned);
```

The is operator does not consider custom or numeric conversions, but it does consider *unboxing conversions* (see "The object Type" on page 78).

Virtual Function Members

A function marked as **virtual** can be *overridden* by subclasses wanting to provide a specialized implementation. Methods, properties, indexers, and events can all be declared **virtual**:

```
public class Asset
{
  public string Name;
  public virtual decimal Liability { get { return 0; } }
}
```

A subclass overrides a virtual method by applying the **override** modifier:

```
public class House : Asset
{
  public decimal Mortgage;

  public override decimal Liability
    { get { return Mortgage; } }
}
```

By default, the Liability of an Asset is 0. A Stock does not need to specialize this behavior. However, the House specializes the Liability property to return the value of the Mortgage:

```
House mansion = new House { Name="Mansion",
                            Mortgage=250000 };
Asset a = mansion;
Console.WriteLine (mansion.Liability); // 250000
Console.WriteLine (a.Liability);       // 250000
```

The signatures, return types, and accessibility of the virtual and overridden methods must be identical. An overridden method can call its base class implementation via the **base** keyword (see "The base Keyword" on page 75).

Abstract Classes and Abstract Members

A class declared as *abstract* can never be instantiated. Instead, only its concrete *subclasses* can be instantiated.

Abstract classes are able to define *abstract members*. Abstract members are like virtual members, except they don't provide a default implementation. That implementation must be provided by the subclass, unless that subclass is also declared abstract:

```
public abstract class Asset
{
  // Note empty implementation
  public abstract decimal NetValue { get; }
}
```

Subclasses override abstract members just as though they were virtual.

Hiding Inherited Members

A base class and a subclass may define identical members. For example:

```
public class A       { public int Counter = 1; }
public class B : A   { public int Counter = 2; }
```

The Counter field in class B is said to *hide* the Counter field in class A. Usually, this happens by accident, when a member is added to the base type *after* an identical member was added to the subtype. For this reason, the compiler generates a warning, and then resolves the ambiguity as follows:

- References to A (at compile time) bind to **A.Counter**.
- References to B (at compile time) bind to **B.Counter**.

Occasionally, you want to hide a member deliberately, in which case you can apply the new modifier to the member in the subclass. The new modifier *does nothing more than suppress the compiler warning that would otherwise result*:

```
public class A     { public     int Counter = 1; }
public class B : A { public new int Counter = 2; }
```

The new modifier communicates your intent to the compiler—and other programmers—that the duplicate member is not an accident.

Sealing Functions and Classes

An overridden function member may *seal* its implementation with the **sealed** keyword to prevent it from being overridden by further subclasses. In our earlier virtual function member example, we could have sealed **House**'s implementation of **Liability**, preventing a class that derives from **House** from over-riding **Liability**, as follows:

```
public sealed override decimal Liability { get { ... } }
```

You can also seal the class itself, implicitly sealing all the virtual functions, by applying the **sealed** modifier to the class itself.

The base Keyword

The base keyword is similar to the **this** keyword. It serves two essential purposes: accessing an overridden function member from the subclass, and calling a base class constructor (see next section).

In this example, **House** uses the **base** keyword to access **Asset**'s implementation of **Liability**:

```
public class House : Asset
{
  ...
```

```
   public override decimal Liability
   {
     get { return base.Liability + Mortgage; }
   }
}
```

With the base keyword, we access Asset's Liability property *nonvirtually*. This means we will always access Asset's version of this property—regardless of the instance's actual runtime type.

The same approach works if Liability is *hidden* rather than *overridden*. (You can also access hidden members by casting to the base class before invoking the function.)

Constructors and Inheritance

A subclass must declare its own constructors. For example, if we define Baseclass and Subclass as follows:

```
public class Baseclass
{
  public int X;
  public Baseclass () { }
  public Baseclass (int x) { this.X = x; }
}
public class Subclass : Baseclass { }
```

the following is illegal:

```
Subclass s = new Subclass (123);
```

Subclass must "redefine" any constructors it wants to expose. In doing so, it can call any of the base class's constructors with the base keyword:

```
public class Subclass : Baseclass
{
  public Subclass (int x) : base (x) { ... }
}
```

The base keyword works rather like the this keyword, except that it calls a constructor in the base class. Base class constructors always execute first; this ensures that *base* initialization occurs before *specialized* initialization.

If a constructor in a subclass omits the **base** keyword, the base type's *parameterless* constructor is implicitly called (if the base class has no parameterless constructor, the compiler generates an error).

Constructor and field initialization order

When an object is instantiated, initialization takes place in the following order:

1. From subclass to base class:
   a. Fields are initialized.
   b. Arguments to base-class constructor calls are evaluated.
2. From base class to subclass:
   a. Constructor bodies execute.

Overloading and Resolution

Inheritance has an interesting impact on method overloading. Consider the following two overloads:

```
static void Foo (Asset a) { }
static void Foo (House h) { }
```

When an overload is called, the most specific type has precedence:

```
House h = new House (...);
Foo(h);                     // Calls Foo(House)
```

The particular overload to call is determined statically (at compile time) rather than at runtime. The following code calls Foo(Asset), even though the runtime type of a is House:

```
Asset a = new House (...);
Foo(a);                     // Calls Foo(Asset)
```

The object Type

object (System.Object) is the ultimate base class for all types.
Any type can be implicitly upcast to object.

To illustrate how this is useful, consider a general-purpose
stack. A stack is a data structure based on the principle of
LIFO—"Last In, First Out." A stack has two operations:
push an object on the stack, and *pop* an object off the stack.
Here is a simple implementation that can hold up to 10 objects:

```
public class Stack
{
  int position;
  object[] data = new object[10];
  public void Push (object o) { data[position++] = o; }
  public object Pop() { return data[--position]; }
}
```

Because Stack works with the object type, we can Push and
Pop instances of *any type* to and from the Stack:

```
Stack stack = new Stack();
stack.Push ("sausage");
string s = (string) stack.Pop();   // Downcast
Console.WriteLine (s);             // sausage
```

object is a reference type, by virtue of being a class. Despite
this, value types, such as int, can also be cast to and from
object. To make this possible, the CLR must perform some
special work to bridge the underlying differences between
value and reference types. This process is called *boxing* and
unboxing.

Boxing and Unboxing

Boxing is the act of casting a value-type instance to a reference-type instance. The reference type may be either the **object** class or an interface (see "Interfaces" on page 85). In this example, we box an **int** into an object:

```
int x = 9;
object obj = x;          // Box the int
```

Unboxing reverses the operation, by casting the object back to the original value type:

```
int y = (int)obj;        // Unbox the int
```

Unboxing requires an explicit cast. The runtime checks that the stated value type matches the actual object type, and throws an **InvalidCastException** if the check fails. For instance, the following throws an exception, because **long** does not exactly match **int**:

```
object obj = 9;          // 9 is inferred to be of type int
long x = (long) obj;     // InvalidCastException
```

The following succeeds, however:

```
object obj = 9;
long x = (int) obj;
```

As does this:

```
object obj = 3.5;        // 3.5 inferred to be type double
int x = (int) (double) obj;   // x is now 3
```

In the last example, **(double)** performs an *unboxing* and then **(int)** performs a *numeric conversion*.

Unlike with reference conversions, boxing *copies* the value-type instance into the new object, and unboxing *copies* the contents of the object back into a value-type instance:

```
int i = 3;
object boxed = i;
i = 5;
Console.WriteLine (boxed);    // 3
```

Static and Runtime Type Checking

C# checks types both statically (at compile time) and at runtime.

Static type checking enables the compiler to verify the correctness of your program without running it. The following code will fail because the compiler enforces static typing:

```
int x = "5";
```

Runtime type checking is performed by the CLR when you downcast via a reference conversion or unboxing:

```
object y = "5";
int z = (int) y;       // Runtime error, downcast failed
```

Runtime type checking is possible because each object on the heap internally stores a little type token. This token can be retrieved by calling the GetType method of object.

The GetType Method and typeof Operator

All types in C# are represented at runtime with an instance of System.Type. There are two basic ways to get a System.Type object: call GetType on the instance, or use the typeof operator on a type name. GetType is evaluated at runtime; typeof is evaluated statically at compile time.

System.Type has properties for such things as the type's name, assembly, base type, and so on. For example:

```
int x = 3;

Console.Write (x.GetType().Name);           // Int32
Console.Write (typeof(int).Name);           // Int32
Console.Write (x.GetType().FullName);    // System.Int32
Console.Write (x.GetType() == typeof(int));    // True
```

System.Type also has methods that act as a gateway to the run-time's reflection model. For detailed information, see Chapter 18 of *C# 4.0 in a Nutshell* (O'Reilly).

Object Member Listing

Here are all the members of object:

```
public extern Type GetType();
public virtual bool Equals (object obj);
public static bool Equals (object objA, object objB);
public static bool ReferenceEquals (object objA,
                                    object objB);
public virtual int GetHashCode();
public virtual string ToString();
protected override void Finalize();
protected extern object MemberwiseClone();
```

Equals, ReferenceEquals, and GetHashCode

The Equals method in the object class is similar to the == operator, except that Equals is virtual, whereas == is static. The following example illustrates the difference:

```
object x = 3;
object y = 3;
Console.WriteLine (x == y);         // False
Console.WriteLine (x.Equals (y));  // True
```

Because x and y have been cast to the object type, the compiler statically binds to object's == operator, which uses *reference-type* semantics to compare two instances. (And because x and y are boxed, they are represented in separate memory locations, and so are unequal.) The virtual Equals method, however, defers to the Int32 type's Equals method, which uses *value-type* semantics in comparing two values.

The static `object.Equals` method simply calls the virtual `Equals` method on the first argument—after checking that the arguments are not null:

```
object x = null, y = 3;
bool error = x.Equals (y);        // Runtime error!
bool ok = object.Equals (x, y);   // OK (false)
```

`ReferenceEquals` forces a reference-type equality comparison (this is occasionally useful on reference types where the == operator has been overloaded to do otherwise).

`GetHashCode` emits a hash code suitable for use with hashtable-based dictionaries, namely `System.Collections.Generic.Dictionary` and `System.Collections.Hashtable`.

To customize a type's equality semantics, you must at a minimum override `Equals` and `GetHashCode`. You would also usually overload the == and != operators. For an example on how to do both, see "Operator Overloading" on page 135.

The ToString Method

The `ToString` method returns the default textual representation of a type instance. The `ToString` method is overridden by all built-in types:

```
string s1 = 1.ToString();      // s1 is "1"
string s2 = true.ToString();   // s2 is "True"
```

You can override the `ToString` method on custom types as follows:

```
public override string ToString() { return "Foo"; }
```

Structs

A *struct* is similar to a class, with the following key differences:

- A struct is a value type, whereas a class is a reference type.
- A struct does not support inheritance (other than implicitly deriving from `object`, or more precisely, `System.Value Type`).

A struct can have all the members a class can, except a parameterless constructor, a finalizer, and virtual members.

A struct is used instead of a class when value-type semantics are desirable. Good examples are numeric types, where it is more natural for assignment to copy a value rather than a reference. Because a struct is a value type, each instance does not require instantiation of an object on the heap; this can result in a useful saving when creating many instances of a type. For instance, creating an array of value types requires only a single heap allocation.

Struct Construction Semantics

The construction semantics of a struct are as follows:

- A parameterless constructor that you can't override implicitly exists. This performs a bitwise-zeroing of its fields.
- When you define a struct constructor (with parameters), you must explicitly assign every field.
- You can't have field initializers in a struct.

Access Modifiers

To promote encapsulation, a type or type member may limit its *accessibility* to other types and other assemblies by adding one of five *access modifiers* to the declaration:

`public`
> Fully accessible. This is the implicit accessibility for members of an enum or interface.

`internal`
> Accessible only within containing assembly or friend assemblies. This is default accessibility for non-nested types.

`private`
> Visible only within containing type. This is the default accessibility for members of a class or struct.

```
protected
```
Visible only within containing type or subclasses.

```
protected internal
```
The *union* of `protected` and `internal` accessibility (this is *less* restrictive than `protected` or `internal` alone).

In the following example, `Class2` is accessible from outside its assembly; `Class1` is not:

```
class Class1 {}          // Class1 is internal (default)
public class Class2 {}
```

`ClassB` exposes field `x` to other types in the same assembly; `ClassA` does not:

```
class ClassA { int x;          } // x is private
class ClassB { internal int x; }
```

When overriding a base class function, accessibility must be identical on the overridden function. The compiler prevents any inconsistent use of access modifiers—for example, a subclass itself can be less accessible than a base class, but not more.

Friend Assemblies

In advanced scenarios, you can expose `internal` members to other *friend* assemblies by adding the `System.Runtime.Com pilerServices.InternalsVisibleTo` assembly attribute, specifying the name of the friend assembly as follows:

```
[assembly: InternalsVisibleTo ("Friend")]
```

If the friend assembly is signed with a strong name, you must specify its *full* 160-byte public key. You can extract this key via a LINQ query—an interactive example is given in LINQPad's free sample library for *C# 4.0 in a Nutshell* (O'Reilly).

Accessibility Capping

A type caps the accessibility of its declared members. The most common example of capping is when you have an `internal` type with `public` members. For example:

```
class C { public void Foo() {} }
```

C's (default) `internal` accessibility caps `Foo`'s accessibility, effectively making `Foo` `internal`. A common reason `Foo` would be marked `public` is to make for easier refactoring, should C later be changed to `public`.

Interfaces

An interface is similar to a class, but it provides a specification rather than an implementation for its members. An interface is special in the following ways:

- A class can implement *multiple* interfaces. In contrast, a class can inherit from only a *single* class.
- Interface members are *all implicitly abstract*. In contrast, a class can provide both abstract members and concrete members with implementations.
- *Structs* can implement interfaces, whereas a struct cannot inherit from a class.

An interface declaration is like a class declaration, but it provides no implementation for its members, since all its members are implicitly abstract. These members will be implemented by the classes and structs that implement the interface. An interface can contain only methods, properties, events, and indexers, which not coincidentally, are precisely the members of a class that can be abstract.

Here is a slightly simplified version of the `IEnumerator` interface, defined in `System.Collections`:

```
public interface IEnumerator
{
  bool MoveNext();
  object Current { get; }
}
```

Interface members are always implicitly public and cannot declare an access modifier. Implementing an interface means providing a `public` implementation for all its members:

```
internal class Countdown : IEnumerator
{
  int count = 11;
  public bool MoveNext() { return count-- > 0 ; }
  public object Current  { get { return count; } }
}
```

You can implicitly cast an object to any interface that it implements:

```
IEnumerator e = new Countdown();
while (e.MoveNext())
  Console.Write (e.Current);      // 109876543210
```

Extending an Interface

Interfaces may derive from other interfaces. For instance:

```
public interface IUndoable            { void Undo(); }
public interface IRedoable : IUndoable { void Redo(); }
```

IRedoable inherits all the members of IUndoable.

Explicit Interface Implementation

Implementing multiple interfaces can sometimes result in a collision between member signatures. You can resolve such collisions by *explicitly implementing* an interface member. For example:

```
interface I1 { void Foo(); }
interface I2 { int Foo();  }

public class Widget : I1, I2
{
  public void Foo()   // Implicit implementation
  {
    Console.Write ("Widget's implementation of I1.Foo");
  }

  int I2.Foo()   // Explicit implementation of I2.Foo
  {
    Console.Write ("Widget's implementation of I2.Foo");
    return 42;
  }
}
```

Because both `I1` and `I2` have conflicting `Foo` signatures, `Widget` explicitly implements `I2`'s `Foo` method. This lets the two methods coexist in one class. The only way to call an explicitly implemented member is to cast to its interface:

```
Widget w = new Widget();
w.Foo();          // Widget's implementation of I1.Foo
((I1)w).Foo();    // Widget's implementation of I1.Foo
((I2)w).Foo();    // Widget's implementation of I2.Foo
```

Another reason to explicitly implement interface members is to hide members that are highly specialized and distracting to a type's normal use case. For example, a type that implements `ISerializable` would typically want to avoid flaunting its `ISerializable` members unless explicitly cast to that interface.

Implementing Interface Members Virtually

An implicitly implemented interface member is, by default, sealed. It must be marked `virtual` or `abstract` in the base class in order to be overridden: calling the interface member through either the base class or the interface then calls the subclass's implementation.

An explicitly implemented interface member cannot be marked `virtual`, nor can it be overridden in the usual manner. It can, however, be *reimplemented*.

Reimplementing an Interface in a Subclass

A subclass can *reimplement* any interface member already implemented by a base class. Reimplementation hijacks a member implementation (when called through the interface) and works whether or not the member is `virtual` in the base class.

In the following example, `TextBox` implements `IUndo.Undo` explicitly, and so it cannot be marked as `virtual`. In order to "override" it, `RichTextBox` must reimplement `IUndo`'s `Undo` method:

```
public interface IUndoable { void Undo(); }

public class TextBox : IUndoable
{
  void IUndoable.Undo()
    { Console.WriteLine ("TextBox.Undo"); }
}

public class RichTextBox : TextBox, IUndoable
{
  public new void Undo()
    { Console.WriteLine ("RichTextBox.Undo"); }
}
```

Calling the reimplemented member through the interface calls the subclass's implementation:

```
RichTextBox r = new RichTextBox();
r.Undo();                  // RichTextBox.Undo
((IUndoable)r).Undo();     // RichTextBox.Undo
```

In this case, Undo is implemented explicitly. Implicitly implemented members can also be reimplemented, but the effect is nonpervasive, in that calling the member through the base class invokes the base implementation.

Enums

An enum is a special value type that lets you specify a group of named numeric constants. For example:

```
public enum BorderSide { Left, Right, Top, Bottom }
```

We can use this enum type as follows:

```
BorderSide topSide = BorderSide.Top;
bool isTop = (topSide == BorderSide.Top);   // true
```

Each enum member has an underlying integral value. By default, the underlying values are of type int, and the enum members are assigned the constants 0, 1, 2... (in their declaration order). You may specify an alternative integral type, as follows:

```
public enum BorderSide : byte { Left, Right, Top, Bottom }
```

You may also specify an explicit integral value for each member:

```
public enum BorderSide : byte
  { Left=1, Right=2, Top=10, Bottom=11 }
```

The compiler also lets you explicitly assign *some* of the enum members. The unassigned enum members keep incrementing from the last explicit value. The preceding example is equivalent to:

```
public enum BorderSide : byte
  { Left=1, Right, Top=10, Bottom }
```

Enum Conversions

You can convert an **enum** instance to and from its underlying integral value with an explicit cast:

```
int i = (int) BorderSide.Left;
BorderSide side = (BorderSide) i;
bool leftOrRight = (int) side <= 2;
```

You can also explicitly cast one enum type to another; the translation then uses the members' underlying integral values.

The numeric literal **0** is treated specially in that it does not require an explicit cast:

```
BorderSide b = 0;      // No cast required
if (b == 0) ...
```

In this particular example, **BorderSide** has no member with an integral value of **0**. This does not generate an error: a limitation of enums is that the compiler and CLR do not prevent the assignment of integrals whose values fall outside the range of members:

```
BorderSide b = (BorderSide) 12345;
Console.WriteLine (b);                    // 12345
```

Flags Enums

You can combine enum members. To prevent ambiguities, members of a combinable enum require explicitly assigned values, typically in powers of two. For example:

```
[Flags]
public enum BorderSides
  { Left=1, Right=2, Top=4, Bottom=8 }
```

By convention, a combinable enum type is given a plural rather than singular name. To work with combined enum values, you use bitwise operators, such as | and &. These operate on the underlying integral values:

```
BorderSides leftRight =
  BorderSides.Left | BorderSides.Right;

if ((leftRight & BorderSides.Left) != 0)
  Console.WriteLine ("Includes Left");   // Includes Left

string formatted = leftRight.ToString(); // "Left, Right"

BorderSides s = BorderSides.Left;
s |= BorderSides.Right;
Console.WriteLine (s == leftRight);        // True
```

The Flags attribute should be applied to combinable enum types; if you fail to do this, calling ToString on an enum instance emits a number rather than a series of names.

For convenience, you can include combination members within an enum declaration itself:

```
[Flags] public enum BorderSides
{
  Left=1, Right=2, Top=4, Bottom=8,
  LeftRight = Left | Right,
  TopBottom = Top  | Bottom,
  All       = LeftRight | TopBottom
}
```

Enum Operators

The operators that work with enums are:

```
=    ==   !=   <    >    <=   >=   +    -    ^    &    |    ~
+=   -=   ++   -    sizeof
```

The bitwise, arithmetic, and comparison operators return the result of processing the underlying integral values. Addition is permitted between an enum and an integral type, but not between two enums.

Nested Types

A *nested type* is declared within the scope of another type. For example:

```
public class TopLevel
{
  public class Nested { }             // Nested class
  public enum Color { Red, Blue, Tan } // Nested enum
}
```

A nested type has the following features:

- It can access the enclosing type's private members and everything else the enclosing type can access.
- It can be declared with the full range of access modifiers, rather than just public and internal.
- The default visibility for a nested type is private rather than internal.
- Accessing a nested type from outside the enclosing type requires qualification with the enclosing type's name (like when accessing static members).

For example, to access Color.Red from outside our TopLevel class, we'd have to do this:

```
TopLevel.Color color = TopLevel.Color.Red;
```

All types can be nested; however, only classes and structs can *nest*.

Generics

C# has two separate mechanisms for writing code that is reusable across different types: *inheritance* and *generics*. Whereas inheritance expresses reusability with a base type, generics express reusability with a "template" that contains "placeholder" types. Generics, when compared to inheritance, can *increase type safety* and *reduce casting and boxing*.

Generic Types

A generic type declares *type parameters*—placeholder types to be filled in by the consumer of the generic type, which supplies the *type arguments*. Here is a generic type, Stack<T>, designed to stack instances of type T. Stack<T> declares a single type parameter T:

```
public class Stack<T>
{
  int position;
  T[] data = new T[100];
  public void Push (T obj) { data[position++] = obj;  }
  public T Pop()           { return data[--position]; }
}
```

We can use Stack<T> as follows:

```
Stack<int> stack = new Stack<int>();
stack.Push(5);
stack.Push(10);
int x = stack.Pop();      // x is 10
int y = stack.Pop();      // y is 5
```

NOTE

Notice that no downcasts are required in the last two lines, avoiding the possibility of runtime error and eliminating the overhead of boxing/unboxing. This makes our generic stack superior to a nongeneric stack that uses object in place of T (see "The object Type" on page 78 for an example).

Stack<int> fills in the type parameter T with the type argument int, implicitly creating a type on the fly (the synthesis occurs at runtime). Stack<int> effectively has the following definition (substitutions appear in bold, with the class name hashed out to avoid confusion):

```
public class ###
{
  int position;
  int[] data;
  public void Push (int obj) { data[position++] = obj;  }
  public int Pop()          { return data[--position]; }
}
```

Technically, we say that Stack<T> is an *open type*, whereas Stack<int> is a *closed type*. At runtime, all generic type instances are closed—with the placeholder types filled in.

Generic Methods

A generic method declares type parameters within the signature of a method. With generic methods, many fundamental algorithms can be implemented in a general-purpose way only. Here is a generic method that swaps two values of any type:

```
static void Swap<T> (ref T a, ref T b)
{
  T temp = a; a = b; b = temp;
}
```

Swap<T> can be used as follows:

```
int x = 5, y = 10;
Swap (ref x, ref y);
```

Generally, there is no need to supply type arguments to a generic method, because the compiler can implicitly infer the type. If there is ambiguity, generic methods can be called with the type arguments as follows:

```
Swap<int> (ref x, ref y);
```

Within a generic *type*, a method is not classed as generic unless it *introduces* type parameters (with the angle bracket syntax). The Pop method in our generic stack merely consumes the type's existing type parameter, T, and is not classed as a generic method.

Methods and types are the only constructs that can introduce type parameters. Properties, indexers, events, fields, constructors, operators, and so on cannot declare type parameters, although they can partake in any type parameters already declared by their enclosing type. In our generic stack example, for instance, we could write an indexer that returns a generic item:

```
public T this [int index] { get { return data[index]; } }
```

Similarly, constructors can partake in existing type parameters, but not *introduce* them.

Declaring Type Parameters

Type parameters can be introduced in the declaration of classes, structs, interfaces, delegates (see the section "Delegates" on page 100), and methods. A generic type or method can have multiple parameters:

```
class Dictionary<TKey, TValue> {...}
```

To instantiate:

```
var myDic = new Dictionary<int,string>();
```

Generic type names and method names can be overloaded as long as the number of type parameters differs. For example, the following two type names do not conflict:

```
class A<T> {}
class A<T1,T2> {}
```

NOTE

By convention, generic types and methods with a *single* type parameter name their parameter T, as long as the intent of the parameter is clear. With *multiple* type parameters, each parameter has a more descriptive name (prefixed by T).

---

typeof and Unbound Generic Types

Open generic types do not exist at runtime: open generic types are closed as part of compilation. However, it is possible for an *unbound* generic type to exist at runtime—purely as a **Type** object. The only way to specify an unbound generic type in C# is with the **typeof** operator:

```
class A<T> {}
class A<T1,T2> {}
...

Type a1 = typeof (A<>);    // Unbound type
Type a2 = typeof (A<,>);   // Indicates 2 type args
Console.Write (a2.GetGenericArguments().Count());  // 2
```

You can also use the **typeof** operator to specify a closed type:

```
Type a3 = typeof (A<int,int>);
```

or an open type (which is closed at runtime):

```
class B<T> { void X() { Type t = typeof (T); } }
```

The default Generic Value

The **default** keyword can be used to get the default value given a generic type parameter. The default value for a reference type is **null**, and the default value for a value type is the result of bitwise-zeroing the type's fields:

```
static void Zap<T> (T[] array)
{
  for (int i = 0; i < array.Length; i++)
    array[i] = default(T);
}
```

Generic Constraints

By default, a type parameter can be substituted with any type whatsoever. *Constraints* can be applied to a type parameter to require more specific type arguments. There are six kinds of constraint:

```
where T : base-class    // Base class constraint
where T : interface     // Interface constraint
where T : class         // Reference-type constraint
where T : struct        // Value-type constraint
where T : new()         // Parameterless constructor
                        // constraint
where U : T             // Naked type constraint
```

In the following example, GenericClass<T,U> requires T to derive from SomeClass and implement Interface1, and requires U to provide a parameterless constructor:

```
class      SomeClass {}
interface Interface1 {}

class GenericClass<T,U> where T : SomeClass, Interface1
                        where U : new()
{ ... }
```

Constraints can be applied wherever type parameters are defined, whether in methods or type definitions.

A *base class constraint* specifies that the type parameter must subclass (or match) a particular class; an *interface constraint* specifies that the type parameter must implement that interface. These constraints allow instances of the type parameter to be implicitly converted to that class or interface.

The *class constraint* and *struct constraint* specify that T must be a reference type or a (non-nullable) value type, respectively. The *parameterless constructor constraint* requires T to have a public parameterless constructor and allows you to call new() on T:

```
static void Initialize<T> (T[] array) where T : new()
{
  for (int i = 0; i < array.Length; i++)
    array[i] = new T();
}
```

The *naked type constraint* requires one type parameter to derive from (or match) another type parameter.

Subclassing Generic Types

A generic class can be subclassed just like a nongeneric class. The subclass can leave the base class's type parameters open, as in the following example:

```
class Stack<T>                       {...}
class SpecialStack<T> : Stack<T> {...}
```

Or the subclass can close the generic type parameters with a concrete type:

```
class IntStack : Stack<int>   {...}
```

A subtype can also introduce fresh type arguments:

```
class List<T>                        {...}
class KeyedList<T,TKey> : List<T> {...}
```

Self-Referencing Generic Declarations

A type can name *itself* as the concrete type when closing a type argument:

```
public interface IEquatable<T> { bool Equals (T obj); }

public class Balloon : IEquatable<Balloon>
{
  public bool Equals (Balloon b) { ... }
}
```

The following are also legal:

```
class Foo<T> where T : IComparable<T> { ... }
class Bar<T> where T : Bar<T> { ... }
```

Static Data

Static data is unique for each closed type:

```
class Bob<T> { public static int Count; }
...
Console.WriteLine (++Bob<int>.Count);    // 1
Console.WriteLine (++Bob<int>.Count);    // 2
Console.WriteLine (++Bob<string>.Count); // 1
Console.WriteLine (++Bob<object>.Count); // 1
```

Covariance (C# 4.0)

NOTE

Covariance and contravariance are advanced concepts. The motivation behind their introduction into C# 4.0 was to allow generic interfaces and generics (in particular, those defined in the Framework, such as IEnumerable<T>) to work *more as you'd expect*. You can benefit from this without understanding the details behind covariance and contravariance.

Assuming S subclasses B, type X is *covariant* for its type parameter if X<S> allows a conversion to X<B>. In other words, type IFoo<T> is covariant for T if the following is legal:

```
IFoo<string> s = ...;
IFoo<object> b = s;
```

As of C# 4.0, generic interfaces permit covariance for type parameters marked with the **out** modifier (as do generic delegates). To illustrate, suppose that the Stack<T> class that we wrote at the start of this section implements the following interface:

```
public interface IPoppable<out T> { T Pop(); }
```

The **out** modifier on T indicates that T is used only in *output positions* (e.g., return types for methods). The **out** modifier flags the interface as *covariant* and allows us to do this:

```
// Assuming that Bear subclasses Animal:
var bears = new Stack<Bear>();
bears.Push (new Bear());

// Because bears implements IPoppable<Bear>,
// we can convert it to IPoppable<Animal>:
IPoppable<Animal> animals = bears;   // Legal
Animal a = animals.Pop();
```

The cast from **bears** to **animals** is permitted by the compiler—by virtue of the interface being covariant.

The compiler will generate an error if you use a covariant type parameter in an *input* position (e.g., a parameter to a method or a writable property). The purpose of this limitation is to guarantee compile-time type safety. For instance, it prevents us from adding a Push(T) method to that interface which consumers could abuse with the seemingly benign operation of pushing a camel onto an IPoppable<Animal> (remember that the underlying type in our example is a stack of bears). In order to define a Push(T) method, T must in fact be *contravariant*.

Contravariance (C# 4.0)

We just saw that a type X is covariant for its type parameter if X<S> allows a conversion to X<B> where S subclasses B. A type is *contravariant* when you can convert in the reverse direction—from X<B> to X<S>. This is supported on interfaces and delegates when the type parameter only appears in *input* positions, designated with the in modifier. Extending our previous example, if the Stack<T> class implements the following interface:

```
public interface IPushable<in T> { void Push (T obj); }
```

we can legally do this:

```
IPushable<Animal> animals = new Stack<Animal>();
IPushable<Bear> bears = animals;    // Legal
bears.Push (new Bear());
```

Mirroring covariance, the compiler will report an error if you try to use a contravariant type parameter in an output position (e.g., as a return value, or in a readable property).

Delegates

A delegate dynamically wires up a method caller to its target method. There are two aspects to a delegate: *type* and *instance*. A *delegate type* defines a *protocol* to which the caller and target will conform, comprising a list of parameter types and a return type. A *delegate instance* is an object that refers to one or more target methods conforming to that protocol.

A delegate instance literally acts as a delegate for the caller: the caller invokes the delegate, and then the delegate calls the target method. This indirection decouples the caller from the target method.

A delegate type declaration is preceded by the keyword `dele gate`, but otherwise it resembles an (abstract) method declaration. For example:

```
delegate int Transformer (int x);
```

To create a delegate instance, you can assign a method to a delegate variable:

```
class Test
{
  static void Main()
  {
    Transformer t = Square;  // Create delegate instance
    int result = t(3);       // Invoke delegate
    Console.Write (result);  // 9
  }
  static int Square (int x) { return x * x; }
}
```

Invoking a delegate is just like invoking a method (since the delegate's purpose is merely to provide a level of indirection):

```
t(3);
```

The statement `Transformer t = Square` is shorthand for:

```
Transformer t = new Transformer (Square);
```

And `t(3)` is shorthand for:

```
t.Invoke (3);
```

A delegate is similar to a *callback*, a general term that captures constructs such as C function pointers.

Writing Plug-in Methods with Delegates

A delegate variable is assigned a method *dynamically*. This is useful for writing plug-in methods. In this example, we have a utility method named `Transform` that applies a transform to each element in an integer array. The `Transform` method has a delegate parameter, for specifying a plug-in transform.

```
public delegate int Transformer (int x);

class Util
{
  public static void Transform (int[] values,
                                Transformer t)
  {
    for (int i = 0; i < values.Length; i++)
      values[i] = t (values[i]);
  }
}

class Test
{
  static void Main()
  {
    int[] values = { 1, 2, 3 };
    Util.Transform (values, Square);
    foreach (int i in values)
      Console.Write (i + " ");    // 1 4 9
  }
```

```
    static int Square (int x) { return x * x; }
}
```

Multicast Delegates

All delegate instances have *multicast* capability. This means that a delegate instance can reference not just a single target method, but also a list of target methods. The + and += operators combine delegate instances. For example:

```
SomeDelegate d = SomeMethod1;
d += SomeMethod2;
```

The last line is functionally the same as:

```
d = d + SomeMethod2;
```

Invoking d will now call both SomeMethod1 and SomeMethod2. Delegates are invoked in the order they are added.

The - and -= operators remove the right delegate operand from the left delegate operand. For example:

```
d -= SomeMethod1;
```

Invoking d will now cause only SomeMethod2 to be invoked.

Calling + or += on a delegate variable with a null value is legal, as is calling -= on a delegate variable with a single target (which will result in the delegate instance being null).

NOTE

Delegates are *immutable*, so when you call += or -=, you're in fact creating a *new* delegate instance and assigning it to the existing variable.

If a multicast delegate has a nonvoid return type, the caller receives the return value from the last method to be invoked. The preceding methods are still called, but their return values are discarded. In most scenarios in which multicast delegates are used, they have void return types, so this subtlety does not arise.

All delegate types implicitly derive from `System.MulticastDele`
`gate`, which inherits from `System.Delegate`. C# compiles +, -,
+=, and -= operations made on a delegate to the static `Combine`
and `Remove` methods of the `System.Delegate` class.

Instance Versus Static Method Targets

When a delegate object is assigned to an *instance* method, the
delegate object must maintain a reference not only to the
method, but also to the *instance* to which the method belongs.
The `System.Delegate` class's `Target` property represents this instance (and will be null for a delegate referencing a static
method).

Generic Delegate Types

A delegate type may contain generic type parameters. For
example:

```
public delegate T Transformer<T> (T arg);
```

Here's how we could use this delegate type:

```
static double Square (double x) { return x * x; }

static void Main()
{
  Transformer<double> s = Square;
  Console.WriteLine (s (3.3));        // 10.89
}
```

The Func and Action Delegates

With generic delegates, it becomes possible to write a small set
of delegate types that are so general they can work for methods
of any return type and any (reasonable) number of arguments.
These delegates are the `Func` and `Action` delegates, defined in
the `System` namespace (the `in` and `out` annotations indicate
variance, which we will cover shortly):

```
delegate TResult Func <out TResult> ();
delegate TResult Func <in T, out TResult> (T arg);
```

```
delegate TResult Func <in T1, in T2, out TResult>
  (T1 arg1, T2 arg2);
... and so on, up to T16

delegate void Action ();
delegate void Action <in T> (T arg);
delegate void Action <in T1, in T2> (T1 arg1, T2 arg2);
... and so on, up to T16
```

These delegates are extremely general. The `Transformer` delegate in our previous example can be replaced with a `Func` delegate that takes a single argument of type `T` and returns a same-typed value:

```
public static void Transform<T> (
  T[] values, Func<T,T> transformer)
{
  for (int i = 0; i < values.Length; i++)
    values[i] = transformer (values[i]);
}
```

The only practical scenarios not covered by these delegates are `ref`/`out` and pointer parameters.

Delegate Compatibility

Delegate types are all incompatible with each other, even if their signatures are the same:

```
delegate void D1(); delegate void D2();
...
D1 d1 = Method1;
D2 d2 = d1;               // Compile-time error
```

The following, however, is permitted:

```
D2 d2 = new D2 (d1);
```

Delegate instances are considered equal if they have the same type and method target(s). For multicast delegates, the order of the method targets is significant.

Return type variance

When you call a method, you may get back a type that is more specific than what you asked for. This is ordinary polymorphic behavior. In keeping with this, a delegate target method may return a more specific type than described by the delegate. This is *covariance*, and has been supported since C# 2.0:

```
delegate object ObjectRetriever();
...
static void Main()
{
  ObjectRetriever o = new ObjectRetriever (GetString);
  object result = o();
  Console.WriteLine (result);      // hello
}
static string GetString() { return "hello"; }
```

The `ObjectRetriever` expects to get back an `object`, but an `object` subclass will also do because delegate return types are *covariant*.

Parameter variance

When you call a method, you can supply arguments that have more specific types than the parameters of that method. This is ordinary polymorphic behavior. In keeping with this, a delegate target method may have *less* specific parameter types than described by the delegate. This is called *contravariance*:

```
delegate void StringAction (string s);
...
static void Main()
{
  StringAction sa = new StringAction (ActOnObject);
  sa ("hello");
}
static void ActOnObject (object o)
{
  Console.WriteLine (o);   // hello
}
```

Type parameter variance for generic delegates (C# 4.0)

In "Generics" on page 92, we saw how type parameters can be
covariant and contravariant for generic interfaces. The same
capability also exists for generic delegates in C# 4.0. If you're
defining a generic delegate type, it's good practice to:

- Mark a type parameter used only on the return value as
  covariant (out).

- Mark any type parameters used only on parameters as
  contravariant (in).

Doing so allows conversions to work naturally by respecting
inheritance relationships between types. The following delegate (defined in the System namespace) is covariant for TResult:

```
delegate TResult Func<out TResult>();
```

allowing:

```
Func<string> x = ...;
Func<object> y = x;
```

The following delegate (defined in the System namespace) is
contravariant for T:

```
delegate void Action<in T> (T arg);
```

allowing:

```
Action<object> x = ...;
Action<string> y = x;
```

Events

When using delegates, two emergent roles commonly appear: *broadcaster* and *subscriber*. The *broadcaster* is a type that contains a delegate field. The broadcaster decides when to broadcast, by invoking the delegate. The *subscribers* are the method target recipients. A subscriber decides when to start and stop listening, by calling += and -= on the broadcaster's delegate. A subscriber does not know about, or interfere with, other subscribers.

Events are a language feature that formalizes this pattern. An **event** is a construct that exposes just the subset of delegate features required for the broadcaster/subscriber model. The main purpose of events is to *prevent subscribers from interfering with each other*.

The easiest way to declare an event is to put the **event** keyword in front of a delegate member:

```
public class Broadcaster
{
  public event ProgressReporter Progress;
}
```

Code within the **Broadcaster** type has full access to **Progress** and can treat it as a delegate. Code outside of **Broadcaster** can only perform += and -= operations on the **Progress** event.

In the following example, the **Stock** class fires its **Price Changed** event every time the **Price** of the **Stock** changes:

```
public delegate void PriceChangedHandler
  (decimal oldPrice, decimal newPrice);
public class Stock
{
  string symbol; decimal price;

  public Stock (string symbol) { this.symbol = symbol; }

  public event PriceChangedHandler PriceChanged;
```

```
public decimal Price
{
  get { return price; }
  set
  {
    if (price == value) return;
    // Fire event if invocation list isn't empty:
    if (PriceChanged != null)
      PriceChanged (price, value);
    price = value;
  }
}
}
```

If we remove the event keyword from our example so that
PriceChanged becomes an ordinary delegate field, our example
would give the same results. However, Stock would be less ro-
bust, in that subscribers could do the following things to interfere with each other:

- Replace other subscribers by reassigning PriceChanged
  (instead of using the += operator).
- Clear all subscribers (by setting PriceChanged to null).
- Broadcast to other subscribers by invoking the delegate.

Events can be virtual, overridden, abstract, or sealed. They can
also be static.

Standard Event Pattern

The .NET Framework defines a standard pattern for writing
events. Its purpose is to provide consistency across both
Framework and user code. Here is the preceding example re-
factored with this pattern:

```
public class PriceChangedEventArgs : EventArgs
{
  public readonly decimal LastPrice, NewPrice;

  public PriceChangedEventArgs (decimal lastPrice,
                                decimal newPrice)
  {
    LastPrice = lastPrice; NewPrice = newPrice;
```

```
    }
  }

  public class Stock
  {
    string symbol; decimal price;

    public Stock (string symbol) { this.symbol = symbol; }

    public event EventHandler<PriceChangedEventArgs>
                 PriceChanged;

    protected virtual void OnPriceChanged
                            (PriceChangedEventArgs e)
    {
      if (PriceChanged != null) PriceChanged (this, e);
    }

    public decimal Price
    {
      get { return price; }
      set
      {
        if (price == value) return;
        OnPriceChanged (new PriceChangedEventArgs (price,
                                                   value));
        price = value;
      }
    }
  }
```

At the core of the standard event pattern is System.EventArgs:
a predefined Framework class with no members (other than
the static Empty property). EventArgs is a base class for convey-
ing information for an event. In this example, we subclass
EventArgs to convey the old and new prices when a Price
Changed event is fired.

The generic System.EventHandler delegate is also part of
the .NET Framework and is defined as follows:

```
public delegate void EventHandler<TEventArgs>
  (object source, TEventArgs e)
   where TEventArgs : EventArgs;
```

A protected virtual method, named On-event-name, centralizes firing of the event. This allows subclasses to fire the event (which is usually desirable) and also allows subclasses to insert code before and after the event is fired.

Here's how we could use our Stock class:

```
static void Main()
{
  Stock stock = new Stock ("THPW");
  stock.Price = 27.10M;

  stock.PriceChanged += stock_PriceChanged;
  stock.Price = 31.59M;
}

static void stock_PriceChanged
  (object sender, PriceChangedEventArgs e)
{
  if ((e.NewPrice - e.LastPrice) / e.LastPrice > 0.1M)
    Console.WriteLine ("Alert, 10% price increase!");
}
```

For events that don't carry additional information, the Framework also provides a nongeneric EventHandler delegate. We can demonstrate this by rewriting our Stock class such that the PriceChanged event fires *after* the price changes. This means that no additional information need be transmitted with the event:

```
public class Stock
{
```

```
string symbol; decimal price;

public Stock (string symbol) {this.symbol = symbol;}

public event EventHandler PriceChanged;

protected virtual void OnPriceChanged (EventArgs e)
{
  if (PriceChanged != null) PriceChanged (this, e);
}

public decimal Price
{
  get { return price; }
  set
  {
    if (price == value) return;
    price = value;
    OnPriceChanged (EventArgs.Empty);
  }
}
}
```

Note that we also used the EventArgs.Empty property—this
saves instantiating an instance of EventArgs.

Event Accessors

An event's *accessors* are the implementations of its += and -=
functions. By default, accessors are implemented implicitly by
the compiler. Consider this event declaration:

```
public event EventHandler PriceChanged;
```

The compiler converts this to the following:

- A private delegate field.
- A public pair of event accessor functions, whose implementations forward the += and -= operations to the private
  delegate field.

You can take over this process by defining *explicit* event accessors. Here's a manual implementation of the PriceChanged
event from our previous example:

```
EventHandler _priceChanged;    // Private delegate

public event EventHandler PriceChanged
{
  add    { _priceChanged += value; }
  remove { _priceChanged -= value; }
}
```

This example is functionally identical to C#'s default accessor implementation (except that C# also ensures thread safety around updating the delegate). By defining event accessors ourselves, we instruct C# not to generate default field and accessor logic.

With explicit event accessors, you can apply more complex strategies to the storage and access of the underlying delegate. This is useful when the event accessors are merely relays for another class that is broadcasting the event, or when explicitly implementing an interface that declares an event:

```
public interface IFoo { event EventHandler Ev; }
class Foo : IFoo
{
  EventHandler ev;
  event EventHandler IFoo.Ev
  {
    add { ev += value; } remove { ev -= value; }
  }
}
```

Lambda Expressions

A lambda expression is an unnamed method written in place of a delegate instance. The compiler immediately converts the lambda expression to either:

- A delegate instance.
- An *expression tree*, of type Expression<TDelegate>, representing the code inside the lambda expression in a traversable object model. This allows the lambda expression to be interpreted later at runtime; we describe the process in Chapter 8 of *C# 4.0 in a Nutshell* (O'Reilly).

Given the following delegate type:

```
delegate int Transformer (int i);
```

we could assign and invoke the lambda expression x =>
x * x as follows:

```
Transformer sqr = x => x * x;
Console.WriteLine (sqr(3));    // 9
```

NOTE

Internally, the compiler resolves lambda expressions of
this type by writing a private method, and moving the
expression's code into that method.

A lambda expression has the following form:

```
(parameters) => expression-or-statement-block
```

For convenience, you can omit the parentheses if and only if
there is exactly one parameter of an inferable type.

In our example, there is a single parameter, x, and the expression is x * x:

```
x => x * x;
```

Each parameter of the lambda expression corresponds to a
delegate parameter, and the type of the expression (which may
be void) corresponds to the return type of the delegate.

In our example, x corresponds to parameter i, and the expression x * x corresponds to the return type int, therefore being
compatible with the Transformer delegate.

A lambda expression's code can be a *statement block* instead
of an expression. We can rewrite our example as follows:

```
x => { return x * x; };
```

Lambda expressions are used most commonly with the Func
and Action delegates, so you will most often see our earlier
expression written as follows:

```
Func<int,int> sqr = x => x * x;
```

The compiler can usually *infer* the type of lambda parameters contextually. When this is not the case, you can specify parameter types explicitly:

```
Func<int,int> sqr = (int x) => x * x;
```

Here's an example of an expression that accepts two parameters:

```
Func<string,string,int> totalLength =
 (s1, s2) => s1.Length + s2.Length;

int total = totalLength ("hello", "world");  // total=10;
```

Assuming `Clicked` is an event of type `EventHandler`, the following attaches an event handler via a lambda expression:

```
obj.Clicked += (sender,args) => Console.Write ("Click");
```

Capturing Outer Variables

A lambda expression can reference the local variables and parameters of the method in which it's defined (*outer variables*). For example:

```
static void Main()
{
  int factor = 2;
  Func<int, int> multiplier = n => n * factor;
  Console.WriteLine (multiplier (3));          // 6
}
```

Outer variables referenced by a lambda expression are called *captured variables*. A lambda expression that captures variables is called a *closure*. Captured variables are evaluated when the delegate is actually *invoked*, not when the variables were *captured*:

```
int factor = 2;
Func<int, int> multiplier = n => n * factor;
factor = 10;
Console.WriteLine (multiplier (3));          // 30
```

Lambda expressions can themselves update captured variables:

```
int seed = 0;
Func<int> natural = () => seed++;
Console.WriteLine (natural());        // 0
Console.WriteLine (natural());        // 1
Console.WriteLine (seed);             // 2
```

Captured variables have their lifetimes extended to that of the delegate. In the following example, the local variable **seed** would ordinarily disappear from scope when **Natural** finished executing. But because **seed** has been *captured*, its lifetime is extended to that of the capturing delegate, **natural**:

```
static Func<int> Natural()
{
  int seed = 0;
  return () => seed++;        // Returns a closure
}
static void Main()
{
  Func<int> natural = Natural();
  Console.WriteLine (natural());        // 0
  Console.WriteLine (natural());        // 1
}
```

Capturing iteration variables

When you capture iteration variables in **for** and **foreach** statements, C# treats those iteration variables as though they were declared *outside* the loop. This means that the *same* variable is captured in each iteration. The following program writes 333 instead of writing 012:

```
Action[] actions = new Action[3];

for (int i = 0; i < 3; i++)
  actions [i] = () => Console.Write (i);

foreach (Action a in actions) a();        // 333
```

Each closure (shown in boldface) captures the same variable, i. When the delegates are later invoked, each delegate sees i's value at the time of *invocation*—which is 3. The solution, if we want to write 012, is to assign the iteration variable to a local variable that's scoped *inside* the loop:

```
Action[] actions = new Action[3];
for (int i = 0; i < 3; i++)
{
  int loopScopedi = i;
  actions [i] = () => Console.Write (loopScopedi);
}
foreach (Action a in actions) a();      // 012
```

This then causes the closure to capture a *different* variable on each iteration.

Anonymous Methods

Anonymous methods are a C# 2.0 feature that has been largely subsumed by lambda expressions. An anonymous method is like a lambda expression, except that it lacks implicitly typed parameters, expression syntax (an anonymous method must always be a statement block), and the ability to compile to an expression tree.

To write an anonymous method, you include the `delegate` keyword followed (optionally) by a parameter declaration and then a method body. For example, given this delegate:

```
delegate int Transformer (int i);
```

we could write and call an anonymous method as follows:

```
Transformer sqr = delegate (int x) {return x * x;};
Console.WriteLine (sqr(3));         // 9
```

The first line is semantically equivalent to the following lambda expression:

```
Transformer sqr =        (int x) => {return x * x;};
```

Or simply:

```
Transformer sqr =        x  => x * x;
```

A unique feature of anonymous methods is that you can omit the parameter declaration entirely—even if the delegate expects them. This can be useful in declaring events with a default empty handler:

```
public event EventHandler Clicked = delegate { };
```

This avoids the need for a null check before firing the event. The following is also legal (notice the lack of parameters):

```
Clicked += delegate { Console.Write ("clicked"); };
```

Anonymous methods capture outer variables in the same way lambda expressions do.

try Statements and Exceptions

A **try** statement specifies a code block subject to error-handling or cleanup code. The **try** *block* must be followed by a **catch** *block*, a **finally** *block*, or both. The **catch** block executes when an error occurs in the **try** block. The **finally** block executes after execution leaves the **try** block (or if present, the **catch** block), to perform cleanup code, whether or not an error occurred.

A **catch** block has access to an **Exception** object that contains information about the error. You use a **catch** block to either compensate for the error or *rethrow* the exception. You rethrow an exception if you merely want to log the problem, or if you want to rethrow a new, higher-level exception type.

A **finally** block adds determinism to your program, by always executing no matter what. It's useful for cleanup tasks such as closing network connections.

A **try** statement looks like this:

```
try
{
  ... // exception may get thrown within execution of
      // this block
}
catch (ExceptionA ex)
{
  ... // handle exception of type ExceptionA
}
catch (ExceptionB ex)
{
  ... // handle exception of type ExceptionB
}
```

```
finally
{
  ... // clean-up code
}
```

Consider the following code:

```
int x = 3, y = 0;
Console.WriteLine (x / y);
```

Because y is zero, the runtime throws a DivideByZeroExcep
tion, and our program terminates. We can prevent this by
catching the exception as follows:

```
try
{
  int x = 3, y = 0;
  Console.WriteLine (x / y);
}
catch (DivideByZeroException ex)
{
  Console.Write ("y cannot be zero. ");
}
// Execution resumes here after exception...
```

NOTE

This is a simple example to illustrate exception handling.
We could deal with this particular scenario better in
practice by checking explicitly for the divisor being zero
before calling Calc.

Exceptions are relatively expensive to handle, taking
hundreds of clock cycles.

When an exception is thrown, the CLR performs a test:

*Is execution currently within a try statement that can catch the
exception?*

- If so, execution is passed to the compatible catch block.
  If the catch block successfully finishes executing, execution moves to the next statement after the try statement
  (if present, executing the finally block first).

- If not, execution jumps back to the caller of the function, and the test is repeated (after executing any **finally** blocks that wrap the statement).

If no function in the call stack takes responsibility for the exception, an error dialog is displayed to the user, and the program terminates.

The catch Clause

A catch clause specifies what type of exception to catch. This must either be System.Exception or a subclass of System.Exception. Catching System.Exception catches all possible errors. This is useful when:

- Your program can potentially recover, regardless of the specific exception type.
- You plan to rethrow the exception (perhaps after logging it).
- Your error handler is the last resort, prior to termination of the program.

More typically, though, you catch *specific exception types*, in order to avoid having to deal with circumstances for which your handler wasn't designed (e.g., an OutOfMemoryException).

You can handle multiple exception types with multiple catch clauses:

```
try
{
  DoSomething();
}
catch (IndexOutOfRangeException ex) { ... }
catch (FormatException ex)          { ... }
catch (OverflowException ex)        { ... }
```

Only one catch clause executes for a given exception. If you want to include a safety net to catch more general exceptions (such as System.Exception) you must put the more specific handlers *first*.

An exception can be caught without specifying a variable, if you don't need to access its properties:

```
catch (StackOverflowException)    // no variable
  { ... }
```

Furthermore, you can omit both the variable and the type (meaning that all exceptions will be caught):

```
catch { ... }
```

NOTE

In languages other than C#, it is possible (though not recommended) to throw an object that does not derive from Exception. The CLR automatically wraps that object in a RuntimeWrappedException class (which does derive from Exception).

The finally Block

A finally block always executes—whether or not an exception is thrown and whether or not the try block runs to completion. finally blocks are typically used for cleanup code.

A finally block executes either:

- After a catch block finishes.
- After control leaves the try block because of a jump statement (e.g., return or goto).
- After the try block ends.

A finally block helps add determinism to a program. In the following example, the file that we open *always* gets closed, regardless of whether:

- The try block finishes normally.
- Execution returns early because the file is empty (EndOf Stream).
- An IOException is thrown while reading the file.

For example:

```csharp
static void ReadFile()
{
  StreamReader reader = null;  // In System.IO namespace
  try
  {
    reader = File.OpenText ("file.txt");
    if (reader.EndOfStream) return;
    Console.WriteLine (reader.ReadToEnd());
  }
  finally
  {
    if (reader != null) reader.Dispose();
  }
}
```

In this example, we closed the file by calling `Dispose` on the `StreamReader`. Calling `Dispose` on an object, within a `finally` block, is a standard convention throughout the .NET Framework and is supported explicitly in C# through the `using` statement.

The using statement

Many classes encapsulate unmanaged resources, such as file handles, graphics handles, or database connections. These classes implement `System.IDisposable`, which defines a single parameterless method named `Dispose` to clean up these resources. The `using` statement provides an elegant syntax for calling `Dispose` on an `IDisposable` object within a `finally` block.

The following:

```csharp
using (StreamReader reader = File.OpenText ("file.txt"))
{
  ...
}
```

is precisely equivalent to:

```csharp
StreamReader reader = File.OpenText ("file.txt");
try
{
  ...
```

```
  }
  finally
  {
    if (reader != null) ((IDisposable)reader).Dispose();
  }
```

Throwing Exceptions

Exceptions can be thrown either by the runtime or in user code. In this example, `Display` throws a `System.ArgumentNull Exception`:

```
static void Display (string name)
{
  if (name == null)
    throw new ArgumentNullException ("name");

  Console.WriteLine (name);
}
```

Rethrowing an exception

You can capture and rethrow an exception as follows:

```
try {  ...  }
catch (Exception ex)
{
  // Log error
  ...
  throw;          // Rethrow same exception
}
```

Rethrowing in this manner lets you log an error without *swallowing* it. It also lets you back out of handling an exception should circumstances turn out to be outside what you expected.

NOTE

If we replaced `throw` with `throw ex`, the example would still work, but the `StackTrace` property of the exception would no longer reflect the original error.

The other common scenario is to rethrow a more specific or meaningful exception type:

```
try
{
  ... // parse a date of birth from XML element data
}
catch (FormatException ex)
{
  throw new XmlException ("Invalid date of birth", ex);
}
```

When rethrowing a different exception, you can populate the InnerException property with the original exception to aid debugging. Nearly all types of exceptions provide a constructor for this purpose (such as in our example).

Key Properties of System.Exception

The most important properties of System.Exception are the following:

StackTrace
> A string representing all the methods that are called from the origin of the exception to the **catch** block.

Message
> A string with a description of the error.

InnerException
> The inner exception (if any) that caused the outer exception. This, itself, may have another InnerException.

Common Exception Types

The following exception types are used widely throughout the CLR and .NET Framework. You can throw these yourself or use them as base classes for deriving custom exception types.

System.ArgumentException
> Thrown when a function is called with a bogus argument. This generally indicates a program bug.

`System.ArgumentNullException`

Subclass of **ArgumentException** that's thrown when a function argument is (unexpectedly) `null`.

`System.ArgumentOutOfRangeException`

Subclass of **ArgumentException** that's thrown when a (usually numeric) argument is too big or too small. For example, this is thrown when passing a negative number into a function that accepts only positive values.

`System.InvalidOperationException`

Thrown when the state of an object is unsuitable for a method to successfully execute, regardless of any particular argument values. Examples include reading an unopened file or getting the next element from an enumerator where the underlying list has been modified partway through the iteration.

`System.NotSupportedException`

Thrown to indicate that a particular functionality is not supported. A good example is calling the **Add** method on a collection for which **IsReadOnly** returns **true**.

`System.NotImplementedException`

Thrown to indicate that a function has not yet been implemented.

`System.ObjectDisposedException`

Thrown when the object upon which the function is called has been disposed.

NOTE

In Framework 4.0, *Code contracts* eliminate the need for **ArgumentException** (and its subclasses). Code contracts are covered in Chapter 13 of *C# 4.0 in a Nutshell* (O'Reilly).

Enumeration and Iterators

Enumeration

An *enumerator* is a read-only, forward-only cursor over a *sequence of values*. An enumerator is an object that implements System.Collections.IEnumerator or System.Collections.Generic.IEnumerator<T>.

The foreach statement iterates over an *enumerable* object. An enumerable object is the logical representation of a sequence. It is not itself a cursor, but an object that produces cursors over itself. An enumerable either implements IEnumerable/IEnumerable<T> or has a method named GetEnumerator that returns an *enumerator*.

The enumeration pattern is as follows:

```
class Enumerator    // Typically implements IEnumerator<T>
{
  public IteratorVariableType Current { get {...} }
  public bool MoveNext() {...}
}
class Enumerable    // Typically implements IEnumerable<T>
{
  public Enumerator GetEnumerator() {...}
}
```

Here is the high-level way of iterating through the characters in the word *beer* using a foreach statement:

```
foreach (char c in "beer") Console.WriteLine (c);
```

Here is the low-level way of iterating through the characters in *beer* without using a foreach statement:

```
using (var enumerator = "beer".GetEnumerator())
  while (enumerator.MoveNext())
  {
    var element = enumerator.Current;
    Console.WriteLine (element);
  }
```

If the enumerator implements IDisposable, the foreach statement also acts as a using statement, implicitly disposing the
enumerator object as in the earlier example.

Collection Initializers

You can instantiate and populate an enumerable object in a
single step. For example:

```
using System.Collections.Generic;
...

List<int> list = new List<int> {1, 2, 3};
```

The compiler translates the last line into the following:

```
List<int> list = new List<int>();
list.Add (1); list.Add (2); list.Add (3);
```

This requires that the enumerable object implements the Sys
tem.Collections.IEnumerable interface, and that it has an Add
method that has the appropriate number of parameters for the
call.

Iterators

Whereas a foreach statement is a *consumer* of an enumerator,
an iterator is a *producer* of an enumerator. In this example, we
use an iterator to return a sequence of Fibonacci numbers
(where each number is the sum of the previous two):

```
using System;
using System.Collections.Generic;

class Test
{
  static void Main()
  {
    foreach (int fib in Fibs(6))
      Console.Write (fib + "  ");
  }

  static IEnumerable<int> Fibs(int fibCount)
  {
```

```
    for (int i = 0, prevFib = 1, curFib = 1;
        i < fibCount;
        i++)
    {
        yield return prevFib;
        int newFib = prevFib+curFib;
        prevFib = curFib;
        curFib = newFib;
    }
  }
}
OUTPUT: 1   1   2   3   5   8
```

Whereas a **return** statement expresses "Here's the value you asked me to return from this method," a **yield return** statement expresses "Here's the next element you asked me to yield from this enumerator." On each **yield** statement, control is returned to the caller, but the callee's state is maintained so that the method can continue executing as soon as the caller enumerates the next element. The lifetime of this state is bound to the enumerator, such that the state can be released when the caller has finished enumerating.

NOTE

The compiler converts iterator methods into private classes that implement IEnumerable<T> and/or IEnumerator<T>. The logic within the iterator block is "inverted" and spliced into the MoveNext method and Current property on the compiler-written enumerator class. This means that when you call an iterator method, all you're doing is instantiating the compiler-written class; none of your code actually runs! Your code runs only when you start enumerating over the resultant sequence, typically with a foreach statement.

Iterator Semantics

An iterator is a method, property, or indexer that contains one or more **yield** statements. An iterator must return one of the following four interfaces (otherwise, the compiler will generate an error):

```
System.Collections.IEnumerable
System.Collections.IEnumerator
System.Collections.Generic.IEnumerable<T>
System.Collections.Generic.IEnumerator<T>
```

Iterators that return an *enumerator* interface tend to be used less often. They're useful when writing a custom collection class: typically, you name the iterator GetEnumerator and have your class implement IEnumerable<T>.

Iterators that return an *enumerable* interface are more common—and simpler to use because you don't have to write a collection class. The compiler, behind the scenes, writes a private class implementing IEnumerable<T> (as well as IEnumerator<T>).

Multiple yield statements

An iterator can include multiple yield statements:

```
static void Main()
{
  foreach (string s in Foo())
    Console.Write (s + " ");    // One Two Three
}

static IEnumerable<string> Foo()
{
  yield return "One";
  yield return "Two";
  yield return "Three";
}
```

yield break

The yield break statement indicates that the iterator block should exit early, without returning more elements. We can modify Foo as follows to demonstrate:

```
static IEnumerable<string> Foo (bool breakEarly)
{
  yield return "One";
  yield return "Two";
  if (breakEarly) yield break;
  yield return "Three";
}
```

WARNING

A return statement is illegal in an iterator block—you
must use yield break instead.

Composing Sequences

Iterators are highly composable. We can extend our Fibonacci
example by adding the following method to the class:

```
static IEnumerable<int> EvenNumbersOnly (
  IEnumerable<int> sequence)
{
  foreach (int x in sequence)
    if ((x % 2) == 0)
      yield return x;
}
```

We can then output even Fibonacci numbers as follows:

```
foreach (int fib in EvenNumbersOnly (Fibs (6)))
  Console.Write (fib + " ");   // 2 8
```

Each element is not calculated until the last moment—when
requested by a MoveNext() operation. Figure 5 shows the data
requests and data output over time.

The composability of the iterator pattern is essential in building
LINQ queries.

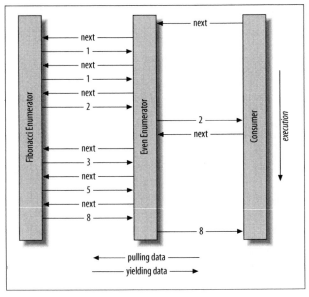

Figure 5. Composing sequences

Nullable Types

Reference types can represent a nonexistent value with a null reference. Value types, however, cannot ordinarily represent null values. For example:

```
string s = null;   // OK - reference type.
int i = null;      // Compile error - int cannot be null.
```

To represent null in a value type, you must use a special construct called a *nullable type*. A nullable type is denoted with a value type followed by the ? symbol:

```
int? i = null;                    // OK - Nullable Type
Console.WriteLine (i == null);    // True
```

Nullable Basics

Nullable<T> struct

T? translates into `System.Nullable<T>`. `Nullable<T>` is a light-weight immutable structure, having only two fields, to represent `Value` and `HasValue`. The essence of `System.Nullable<T>` is very simple:

```
public struct Nullable<T> where T : struct
{
  public T Value {get;}
  public bool HasValue {get;}
  public T GetValueOrDefault();
  public T GetValueOrDefault (T defaultValue);
  ...
}
```

This code:

```
int? i = null;
Console.WriteLine (i == null);          // True
```

translates to:

```
Nullable<int> i = new Nullable<int>();
Console.WriteLine (! i.HasValue);       // True
```

Attempting to retrieve `Value` when `HasValue` is `false` throws an `InvalidOperationException`. `GetValueOrDefault()` returns `Value` if `HasValue` is true; otherwise, it returns `new T()` or a specified custom default value.

The default value of T? is `null`.

Implicit and explicit nullable conversions

The conversion from T to T? is implicit, and from T? to T is explicit. For example:

```
int? x = 5;         // implicit
int y = (int)x;     // explicit
```

The explicit cast is directly equivalent to calling the nullable object's `Value` property. Hence, an `InvalidOperationException` is thrown if `HasValue` is `false`.

Boxing and unboxing nullable values

When T? is boxed, the boxed value on the heap contains T, not T?. This optimization is possible because a boxed value is a reference type that can already express null.

C# also permits the unboxing of nullable types with the **as** operator. The result will be **null** if the cast fails:

```
object o = "string";
int? x = o as int?;
Console.WriteLine (x.HasValue);   // False
```

Operator Lifting

The Nullable<T> struct does not define operators such as <, >, or even ==. Despite this, the following code compiles and executes correctly:

```
int? x = 5;
int? y = 10;
bool b = x < y;      // true
```

This works because the compiler steals or "lifts" the less-than operator from the underlying value type. Semantically, it translates the preceding comparison expression into this:

```
bool b = (x.HasValue && y.HasValue)
           ? (x.Value < y.Value)
           : false;
```

In other words, if both x and y have values, it compares via int's less-than operator; otherwise, it returns **false**.

Operator lifting means you can implicitly use T's operators on T?. You can define operators for T? in order to provide special-purpose null behavior, but in the vast majority of cases, it's best to rely on the compiler automatically applying systematic nullable logic for you.

The compiler performs null logic differently depending on the category of operator.

Equality operators (== and !=)

Lifted equality operators handle nulls just like reference types do. This means two null values are equal:

```
Console.WriteLine (          null ==          null);  // True
Console.WriteLine ((bool?)null == (bool?)null);  // True
```

Further:

- If exactly one operand is null, the operands are unequal.
- If both operands are non-null, their Values are compared.

Relational operators (<, <=, >=, >)

The relational operators work on the principle that it is meaningless to compare null operands. This means comparing a null value to either a null or a non-null value returns false.

```
bool b = x < y;    // Translation:
bool b = (x == null || y == null)
   ? false
   : (x.Value < y.Value);

// b is false (assuming x is 5 and y is null)
```

All other operators (+, −, *, /, %, &, |, ^, <<, >>, +, ++, --, !, ~)

These operators return null when any of the operands are null. This pattern should be familiar to SQL users:

```
int? c = x + y;    // Translation:

int? c = (x == null || y == null)
         ? null
         : (int?) (x.Value + y.Value);

// c is null (assuming x is 5 and y is null)
```

An exception is when the & and | operators are applied to bool?, which we will discuss shortly.

Mixing nullable and nonnullable operators

You can mix and match nullable and nonnullable types (this works because there is an implicit conversion from T to T?):

```
int? a = null;
int b = 2;
int? c = a + b;    // c is null - equivalent to a + (int?)b
```

bool? with & and | Operators

When supplied operands of type bool?, the & and | operators treat null as an *unknown value*. So, null | true is true, because:

- If the unknown value is false, the result would be true.
- If the unknown value is true, the result would be true.

Similarly, null & false is false. This behavior would be familiar to SQL users. The following example enumerates other combinations:

```
bool? n = null, f = false, t = true;
Console.WriteLine (n | n);    // (null)
Console.WriteLine (n | f);    // (null)
Console.WriteLine (n | t);    // True
Console.WriteLine (n & n);    // (null)
Console.WriteLine (n & f);    // False
Console.WriteLine (n & t);    // (null)
```

Null Coalescing Operator

The ?? operator is the null coalescing operator, and it can be used with both nullable types and reference types. It says "If the operand is nonnull, give it to me; otherwise, give me a default value." For example:

```
int? x = null;
int y = x ?? 5;        // y is 5

int? a = null, b = 1, c = 2;
Console.Write (a ?? b ?? c); // 1 (first nonnull value)
```

The ?? operator is equivalent to calling `GetValueOrDefault` with an explicit default value, except that the expression passed to `GetValueOrDefault` is never evaluated if the variable is not null.

Operator Overloading

Operators can be overloaded to provide more natural syntax for custom types. Operator overloading is most appropriately used for implementing custom structs that represent fairly primitive data types. For example, a custom numeric type is an excellent candidate for operator overloading.

The following symbolic operators can be overloaded:

```
+    -    *    /    ++    --    !    ~    %    &    |    ^
==   !=   <    <<   >>    >
```

Implicit and explicit conversions can also be overridden (with the `implicit` and `explicit` keywords), as can the literals `true` and `false`, and the unary + and - operators.

The compound assignment operators (e.g., +=, /=) are automatically overridden when you override the noncompound operators (e.g., +, /).

Operator Functions

An operator is overloaded by declaring an *operator function*. An operator function must be static, and at least one of the operands must be the type in which the operator function is declared.

In the following example, we define a struct called **Note**, representing a musical note, and then overload the + operator:

```csharp
public struct Note
{
  int value;

  public Note (int semitonesFromA)
    { value = semitonesFromA; }
```

```
public static Note operator + (Note x, int semitones)
{
  return new Note (x.value + semitones);
}
}
```

This overload allows us to add an int to a Note:

```
Note B = new Note (2);
Note CSharp = B + 2;
```

Since we overrode +, we can use += too:

```
CSharp += 2;
```

Overloading Equality and Comparison Operators

Equality and comparison operators are often overridden when writing structs, and in rare cases with classes. Special rules and obligations come with overloading these operators:

Pairing

>   The C# compiler enforces that operators that are logical pairs are both defined. These operators are (== !=), (< >), and (<= >=).

Equals *and* GetHashCode

>   If you overload == and !=, you will usually need to override object's Equals and GetHashCode methods, so that collections and hashtables will work reliably with the type.

IComparable *and* IComparable<T>

>   If you overload < and >, you would also typically implement IComparable and IComparable<T>.

Extending the previous example, here's how we could overload Note's equality operators:

```
public static bool operator == (Note n1, Note n2)
{
  return n1.value == n2.value;
}
public static bool operator != (Note n1, Note n2)
{
  return !(n1.value == n2.value);
}
```

```
public override bool Equals (object otherNote)
{
  if (!(otherNote is Note)) return false;
  return this == (Note)otherNote;
}
public override int GetHashCode()
{
  return value.GetHashCode();   // Use value's hashcode
}
```

Custom Implicit and Explicit Conversions

Implicit and explicit conversions are overloadable operators. These conversions are typically overloaded to make converting between strongly related types (such as numeric types) concise and natural.

As explained in the discussion on types, the rationale behind implicit conversions is that they should always succeed and not lose information during conversion. Otherwise, explicit conversions should be defined.

In the following example, we define conversions between our musical Note type and a double (which represents the frequency in hertz of that note):

```
...
// Convert to hertz
public static implicit operator double (Note x)
{
  return 440 * Math.Pow (2,(double) x.value / 12 );
}

// Convert from hertz (accurate to nearest semitone)
public static explicit operator Note (double x)
{
  return new Note ((int) (0.5 + 12 * (Math.Log(x/440)
                  / Math.Log(2)) ));
}
...

Note n =(Note)554.37;  // explicit conversion
double x = n;          // implicit conversion
```

Custom conversions are ignored by the **as** and **is** operators.

Extension Methods

Extension methods allow an existing type to be extended with new methods, without altering the definition of the original type. An extension method is a static method of a static class, where the **this** modifier is applied to the first parameter. The type of the first parameter will be the type that is extended. For example:

```
public static class StringHelper
{
  public static bool IsCapitalized (this string s)
  {
    if (string.IsNullOrEmpty (s)) return false;
    return char.IsUpper (s[0]);
  }
}
```

The IsCapitalized extension method can be called as though it were an instance method on a string, as follows:

```
Console.Write ("Perth".IsCapitalized());
```

An extension method call, when compiled, is translated back into an ordinary static method call:

```
Console.Write (StringHelper.IsCapitalized ("Perth"));
```

Interfaces can be extended, too:

```
public static T First<T> (this IEnumerable<T> sequence)
{
  foreach (T element in sequence)
    return element;
  throw new InvalidOperationException ("No elements!");
}
```

```
...
Console.WriteLine ("Seattle".First());   // S
```

Extension Method Chaining

Extension methods, like instance methods, provide a tidy way
to chain functions. Consider the following two functions:

```
public static class StringHelper
{
  public static string Pluralize (this string s) {...}
  public static string Capitalize (this string s) {...}
}
```

x and y are equivalent and both evaluate to **"Sausages"**, but x
uses extension methods, whereas y uses static methods:

```
string x = "sausage".Pluralize().Capitalize();

string y = StringHelper.Capitalize
             (StringHelper.Pluralize ("sausage"));
```

Ambiguity and Resolution

Namespaces

An extension method cannot be accessed unless the namespace
is in scope (typically imported with a **using** statement).

Extension methods versus instance methods

Any compatible instance method will always take precedence
over an extension method—even when the extension method's
parameters are more specifically type-matched.

Extension methods versus extension methods

If two extension methods have the same signature, the extension method must be called as an ordinary static method to
disambiguate the method to call. If one extension method has
more specific arguments, however, the more specific method
takes precedence.

Anonymous Types

An anonymous type is a simple class created on the fly to store a set of values. To create an anonymous type, you use the new keyword followed by an object initializer, specifying the properties and values the type will contain. For example:

```
var dude = new { Name = "Bob", Age = 1 };
```

The compiler resolves this by writing a private nested type with read-only properties for Name (type string) and Age (type int). You must use the var keyword to reference an anonymous type, because the type's name is compiler-generated.

The property name of an anonymous type can be inferred from an expression that is itself an identifier. For example:

```
int Age = 1;
var dude = new { Name = "Bob", Age };
```

is equivalent to:

```
var dude = new { Name = "Bob", Age = Age };
```

You can create arrays of anonymous types as follows:

```
var dudes = new[]
{
  new { Name = "Bob", Age = 30 },
  new { Name = "Mary", Age = 40 }
};
```

Anonymous types are used primarily when writing LINQ queries.

LINQ

LINQ, or Language Integrated Query, allows you to write structured type-safe queries over local object collections and remote data sources.

LINQ lets you query any collection implementing IEnumerable<>, whether an array, list, XML DOM, or remote data source (such as a table in SQL Server). LINQ offers the benefits

---

of both compile-time type checking and dynamic query composition.

NOTE

A good way to experiment with LINQ is to download LINQPad (*http://www.linqpad.net*). LINQPad lets you interactively query local collections and SQL databases in LINQ without any setup and is preloaded with numerous examples.

LINQ Fundamentals

The basic units of data in LINQ are *sequences* and *elements*. A sequence is any object that implements the generic `IEnumera ble` interface, and an element is each item in the sequence. In the following example, `names` is a sequence, and `Tom`, `Dick`, and `Harry` are elements:

```
string[] names = { "Tom", "Dick", "Harry" };
```

A sequence such as this we call a *local sequence* because it represents a local collection of objects in memory.

A *query operator* is a method that transforms a sequence. A typical query operator accepts an *input sequence* and emits a transformed *output sequence*. In the `Enumerable` class in `Sys tem.Linq`, there are around 40 query operators; all implemented as static extension methods. These are called *standard query operators*.

NOTE

LINQ also supports sequences that can be dynamically fed from a remote data source such as SQL Server. These sequences additionally implement the `IQueryable<>` interface and are supported through a matching set of standard query operators in the `Queryable` class.

A simple query

A query is an expression that transforms sequences with one or more query operators. The simplest query comprises one input sequence and one operator. For instance, we can apply the `Where` operator on a simple array to extract those whose length is at least four characters, as follows:

```
string[] names = { "Tom", "Dick", "Harry" };

IEnumerable<string> filteredNames =
  System.Linq.Enumerable.Where (
    names, n => n.Length >= 4);

foreach (string n in filteredNames)
  Console.Write (n + "|");                    // Dick|Harry|
```

Because the standard query operators are implemented as extension methods, we can call `Where` directly on `names`—as though it were an instance method:

```
IEnumerable<string> filteredNames =
  names.Where (n => n.Length >= 4);
```

(For this to compile, you must import the `System.Linq` namespace with a `using` directive.) The `Where` method in `System.Linq.Enumerable` has the following signature:

```
static IEnumerable<TSource> Where<TSource> (
  this IEnumerable<TSource> source,
  Func<TSource,bool> predicate)
```

`source` is the *input sequence*; `predicate` is a delegate that is invoked on each input *element*. `Where` method includes all elements in the *output sequence*, for which the delegate returns true. Internally, it's implemented with an iterator—here's its source code:

```
foreach (TSource element in source)
  if (predicate (element))
    yield return element;
```

Projecting

Another fundamental query operator is the **Select** method. This transforms (*projects*) each element in the input sequence with a given lambda expression:

```
string[] names = { "Tom", "Dick", "Harry" };

IEnumerable<string> upperNames =
  names.Select (n => n.ToUpper());

foreach (string n in upperNames)
  Console.Write (n + "|");        // TOM|DICK|HARRY|
```

A query can project into an anonymous type:

```
var query = names.Select (n => new {
                                     Name = n,
                                     Length = n.Length
                                   });
foreach (var row in query)
  Console.WriteLine (row);
```

Here's the result:

```
{ Name = Tom, Length = 3 }
{ Name = Dick, Length = 4 }
{ Name = Harry, Length = 5 }
```

Take and Skip

The original ordering of elements within an input sequence is significant in LINQ. Some query operators rely on this behavior, such as **Take**, **Skip**, and **Reverse**. The **Take** operator outputs the first x elements, discarding the rest:

```
int[] numbers  = { 10, 9, 8, 7, 6 };
IEnumerable<int> firstThree = numbers.Take (3);
// firstThree is { 10, 9, 8 }
```

The **Skip** operator ignores the first x elements, and outputs the rest:

```
IEnumerable<int> lastTwo = numbers.Skip (3);
```

Element operators

Not all query operators return a sequence. The *element* operators extract one element from the input sequence; examples are First, Last, Single, and ElementAt:

```
int[] numbers      = { 10, 9, 8, 7, 6 };
int firstNumber    = numbers.First();          // 10
int lastNumber     = numbers.Last();           // 6
int secondNumber   = numbers.ElementAt (2);    // 8
int firstOddNum    = numbers.First (n => n%2 == 1);  // 9
```

All of these operators throw an exception if no elements are present. To get a null/empty return value instead of an exception, use FirstOrDefault, LastOrDefault, SingleOrDefault or ElementAtOrDefault.

The Single and SingleOrDefault methods are equivalent to First and FirstOrDefault except that they throw an exception if there's more than one match. This behavior is useful when querying a database table for a row by primary key.

Aggregation operators

The *aggregation* operators return a scalar value; usually of numeric type. The most commonly used aggregation operators are Count, Min, Max and Average:

```
int[] numbers = { 10, 9, 8, 7, 6 };
int count    = numbers.Count();      // 5
int min      = numbers.Min();        // 6
int max      = numbers.Max();        // 10
double avg   = numbers.Average();    // 8
```

Count accepts an optional predicate, which indicates whether to include a given element. The following counts all even numbers:

```
int evenNums = numbers.Count (n => n % 2 == 0);   // 3
```

The Min, Max and Average operators accept an optional argument that transforms each element prior to it being aggregated:

```
int maxRemainderAfterDivBy5 = numbers.Max
                              (n => n % 5);        // 4
```

The following calculates the root-mean-square of numbers:

```
double rms = Math.Sqrt (numbers.Average (n => n * n));
```

Quantifiers

The *quantifiers* return a bool value. The quantifiers are Contains, Any, All, and SequenceEquals (which compares two sequences):

```
int[] numbers = { 10, 9, 8, 7, 6 };

bool hasTheNumberNine = numbers.Contains (9);    // true
bool hasMoreThanZeroElements = numbers.Any();    // true
bool hasOddNum = numbers.Any (n => n % 2 == 1);  // true
bool allOddNums = numbers.All (n => n % 2 == 1); // false
```

Set operators

The *set* operators accept two same-typed input sequences. Concat appends one sequence to another; Union does the same but with duplicates removed:

```
int[] seq1 = { 1, 2, 3 }, seq2 = { 3, 4, 5 };

IEnumerable<int>
  concat = seq1.Concat (seq2),   // { 1, 2, 3, 3, 4, 5 }
  union  = seq1.Union  (seq2),   // { 1, 2, 3, 4, 5 }
```

The other two operators in this category are Intersect and Except:

```
IEnumerable<int>
  commonality = seq1.Intersect (seq2),   // { 3 }
  difference1 = seq1.Except    (seq2),   // { 1, 2 }
  difference2 = seq2.Except    (seq1);   // { 4, 5 }
```

Deferred Execution

An important feature of many query operators is that they execute not when constructed, but when *enumerated* (in other words, when MoveNext is called on its enumerator). Consider the following query:

```
var numbers = new List<int> { 1 };
numbers.Add (1);
```

```
IEnumerable<int> query = numbers.Select (n => n * 10);
numbers.Add (2);     // Sneak in an extra element

foreach (int n in query)
  Console.Write (n + "|");             // 10|20|
```

The extra number that we sneaked into the list *after* construct-
ing the query is included in the result, because it's not until the
foreach statement runs that any filtering or sorting takes place.
This is called *deferred* or *lazy* evaluation. Deferred execution
decouples query *construction* from query *execution*, allowing
you to construct a query in several steps, as well as making it
possible to query a database without retrieving all the rows to
the client. All standard query operators provide deferred execution, with the following exceptions:

- Operators that return a single element or scalar value (the
  element operators, *aggregation operators* and *quantifiers*)

- The following *conversion* operators:

    ToArray, ToList, ToDictionary, ToLookup

The conversion operators are useful, in part, because they de-
feat lazy evaluation. This can be useful when:

- You want to "freeze" or cache the results at a certain point
  in time.

- You want to avoid re-executing a computationally inten-
  sive query, or a query with a remote data source such as a
  LINQ to SQL table. (A side effect of lazy evaluation is that
  the query gets re-evaluated should you later re-enumerate
  it).

The following example illustrates the **ToList** operator:

```
var numbers = new List<int>() { 1, 2 };

List<int> timesTen = numbers
  .Select (n => n * 10)
  .ToList();     // Executes immediately into a List<int>

numbers.Clear();
Console.WriteLine (timesTen.Count);       // Still 2
```

Standard Query Operators

The standard query operators (as implemented in the System. Linq.Enumerable class) can be divided into 12 categories, summarized in Table 1.

Table 1. Query operator categories

Category	Description	Deferred execution?
Filtering	Returns a subset of elements that satisfy a given condition	Yes
Projecting	Transforms each element with a lambda function, optionally expanding subsequences	Yes
Joining	Meshes elements of one collection with another, using a time-efficient lookup strategy	Yes
Ordering	Returns a reordering of a sequence	Yes
Grouping	Groups a sequence into subsequences.	Yes
Set	Accepts two same-typed sequences, and returns their commonality, sum, or difference	Yes
Element	Picks a single element from a sequence	No
Aggregation	Performs a computation over a sequence, returning a scalar value (typically a number)	No

Category	Description	Deferred execution?
Quantifiers	Performs a computation over a sequence, returning true or false	No
Conversion: Import	Converts a nongeneric sequence to a (queryable) generic sequence	Yes
Conversion: Export	Converts a sequence to an array, list, dictionary, or lookup, forcing immediate evaluation	No
Generation	Manufactures a simple sequence	Yes

Tables 2 through 13 summarize each of the query operators. The operators shown in bold have special support in C# (see "Query Expressions" on page 152).

Table 2. Filtering operators

Method	Description
Where	Returns a subset of elements that satisfy a given condition
Take	Returns the first x elements, and discards the rest
Skip	Ignores the first x elements, and returns the rest
TakeWhile	Emits elements from the input sequence until the given predicate is true
SkipWhile	Ignores elements from the input sequence until the given predicate is true, and then emits the rest
Distinct	Returns a collection that excludes duplicates

Table 3. Projection operators

Method	Description
Select	Transforms each input element with a given lambda expression
SelectMany	Transforms each input element, then flattens and concatenates the resultant subsequences

Table 4. Joining operators

Method	Description
Join	Applies a lookup strategy to match elements from two collections, emitting a flat result set
GroupJoin	As above, but emits a *hierarchical* result set

Table 5. Ordering operators

Method	Description
OrderBy, ThenBy	Returns the elements sorted in ascending order
OrderByDescending, ThenByDescending	Returns the elements sorted in descending order
Reverse	Returns the elements in reverse order

Table 6. Grouping operators

Method	Description
GroupBy	Groups a sequence into subsequences

Table 7. Set operators

Method	Description
Concat	Concatenates two sequences
Union	Concatenates two sequences, removing duplicates
Intersect	Returns elements present in both sequences
Except	Returns elements present in the first, but not the second sequence

Table 8. Element operators

Method	Description
First, FirstOrDefault	Returns the first element in the sequence, or the first element satisfying a given predicate
Last, LastOrDefault	Returns the last element in the sequence, or the last element satisfying a given predicate

Method	Description
Single, SingleOrDefault	Equivalent to First/FirstOrDefault, but throws an exception if there is more than one match
ElementAt, ElementAtOrDefault	Returns the element at the specified position
DefaultIfEmpty	Returns null or default(TSource) if the sequence has no elements

Table 9. Aggregation operators

Method	Description
Count, LongCount	Returns the total number of elements in the input sequence, or the number of elements satisfying a given predicate
Min, Max	Returns the smallest or largest element in the sequence
Sum, Average	Calculates a numeric sum or average over elements in the sequence
Aggregate	Performs a custom aggregation

Table 10. Qualifiers

Method	Description
Contains	Returns true if the input sequence contains the given element
Any	Returns true if any elements satisfy the given predicate
All	Returns true if all elements satisfy the given predicate
SequenceEqual	Returns true if the second sequence has identical elements to the input sequence

Table 11. Conversion operators (import)

Method	Description
OfType	Converts IEnumerable to IEnumerable<T>, discarding wrongly typed elements
Cast	Converts IEnumerable to IEnumerable<T>, throwing an exception if there are any wrongly typed elements

Table 12. Table conversion operators (export)

Method	Description
ToArray	Converts IEnumerable<T> to T[]
ToList	Converts IEnumerable<T> to List<T>
ToDictionary	Converts IEnumerable<T> to Dictionary<TKey,TValue>
ToLookup	Converts IEnumerable<T> to ILookup<TKey,TElement>
AsEnumerable	Downcasts to IEnumerable<T>
AsQueryable	Casts or converts to IQueryable<T>

Table 13. Generation operators

Method	Description
Empty	Creates an empty sequence
Repeat	Creates a sequence of repeating elements
Range	Creates a sequence of integers

In addition to these, Framework 4.0 provides a new **Zip** operator, which enumerates two sequences in step (like a zipper), returning a sequence based on applying a function over each element pair.

Chaining Query Operators

To build more complex queries, you chain query operators together. For example, the following query extracts all strings containing the letter "a," sorts them by length, and then converts the results to uppercase:

```
string[] names = { "Tom","Dick","Harry","Mary","Jay" };

IEnumerable<string> query = names
  .Where   (n => n.Contains ("a"))
  .OrderBy (n => n.Length)
  .Select  (n => n.ToUpper());
```

```
foreach (string name in query)
  Console.Write (name + "|");
```

```
// RESULT: JAY|MARY|HARRY|
```

`Where`, `OrderBy`, and `Select` are all standard query operators that resolve to extension methods in the `Enumerable` class. The `Where` operator emits a filtered version of the input sequence; `OrderBy` emits a sorted version of its input sequence; `Select` emits a sequence where each input element is transformed or *projected* with a given lambda expression (`n.ToUpper()`, in this case). Data flows from left to right through the chain of operators, so the data is first filtered, then sorted, then projected. The end result resembles a production line of conveyor belts, as illustrated in Figure 6.

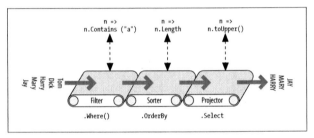

Figure 6. Chaining query operators

Deferred execution is honored throughout with operators, so no filtering, sorting, or projecting takes place until the query is actually enumerated.

Query Expressions

So far, we've written queries by calling extension methods in the `Enumerable` class. In this book, we describe this as *fluent syntax*. C# also provides special language support for writing queries, called *query expressions*. Here's the preceding query expressed as a query expression:

```
using System.Linq;
...
```

```
string[] names = { "Tom","Dick","Harry","Mary","Jay" };

IEnumerable<string> query =
  from n in names
  where n.Contains ("a")
  orderby n.Length
  select n.ToUpper();
```

A query expression always starts with a **from** clause, and ends with either a **select** or **group** clause. The **from** clause declares a *range variable* (in this case, **n**) which you can think of as traversing the input collection—rather like **foreach**. Figure 7 illustrates the complete syntax.

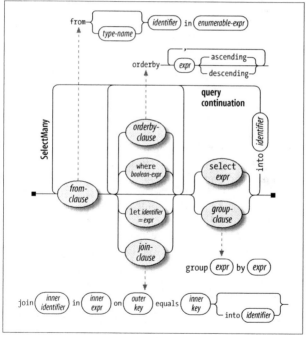

Figure 7. Query expression syntax

The compiler processes query expressions by translating them to fluent syntax. It does this in a fairly mechanical fashion—much like it translates foreach statements into calls to GetEnumerator and MoveNext:

```
IEnumerable<string> query = names
    .Where   (n => n.Contains ("a"))
    .OrderBy (n => n.Length)
    .Select  (n => n.ToUpper());
```

The Where, OrderBy, and Select operators then resolve, using the same rules that would apply if the query were written in fluent syntax. In this case, they bind to extension methods in the Enumerable class (assuming you've imported the System.Linq namespace) because names implements IEnumerable<string>. The compiler doesn't specifically favor the Enumerable class, however, when translating query syntax. You can think of the compiler as mechanically injecting the words "Where," "OrderBy," and "Select" into the statement, and then compiling it as though you'd typed the method names yourself. This offers flexibility in how they resolve—the operators in LINQ to SQL and Entity Framework queries, for instance, bind instead to the extension methods in the Queryable class.

Query expressions versus fluent queries

Query expressions and fluent queries each have advantages.

Query expressions support only a small subset of query operators, namely:

```
Where, Select, SelectMany
OrderBy, ThenBy, OrderByDescending, ThenByDescending
GroupBy, Join, GroupJoin
```

For queries that use other operators, you must either write entirely in fluent syntax or construct mixed-syntax queries, for instance:

```
string[] names = { "Tom","Dick","Harry","Mary","Jay" };

IEnumerable<string> query =
  from   n in names
  where  n.Length == names.Min (n2 => n2.Length)
  select n;
```

This query returns names whose length matches that of the shortest ("Tom" and "Jay"). The subquery (in bold) calculates the minimum length of each name, and evaluates to 3. We have to use fluent syntax for the subquery, because the Min operator has no support in query expression syntax. We can, however, still use query syntax for the outer query.

The main advantage of query syntax is that it can radically simplify queries that involve the following:

- A let clause for introducing a new variable alongside the range variable

- Multiple generators (SelectMany) followed by an outer range variable reference

- A Join or GroupJoin equivalent, followed by an outer range variable reference

The let Keyword

The let keyword introduces a new variable alongside the range variable. For instance, suppose we want to list all names, whose length without vowels, is greater than two characters:

```
string[] names = { "Tom","Dick","Harry","Mary","Jay" };

IEnumerable<string> query =
  from n in names
  let vowelless = Regex.Replace (n, "[aeiou]", "")
  where vowelless.Length > 2
```

```
      orderby vowelless
      select n + " - " + vowelless;
```

The output from enumerating this query is:

```
Dick - Dck
Harry - Hrry
Mary - Mry
```

The **let** clause performs a calculation on each element, without
losing the original element. In our query, the subsequent clauses (**where**, **orderby**, and **select**) have access to both **n** and **vow
elless**. A query can include any multiple **let** clauses, and they
can be interspersed with additional **where** and **join** clauses.

The compiler translates the **let** keyword by projecting into
temporary anonymous type that contains both the original and
transformed elements:

```
IEnumerable<string> query = names
  .Select (n => new
    {
      n = n,
      vowelless = Regex.Replace (n, "[aeiou]", "")
    }
  )
  .Where (temp0 => (temp0.vowelless.Length > 2))
  .OrderBy (temp0 => temp0.vowelless)
  .Select (temp0 => ((temp0.n + " - ") + temp0.vowelless))
```

Query Continuations

If you want to add clauses *after* a **select** or **group** clause, you
must use the **into** keyword to "continue" the query. For
instance:

```
from c in "The quick brown tiger".Split()
select c.ToUpper() into upper
where upper.StartsWith ("T")
select upper

// RESULT: "THE", "TIGER"
```

Following an **into** clause, the previous range variable is out of
scope.

The compiler translates queries with an **into** keyword simply into a longer chain of operators:

```
"The quick brown tiger".Split()
    .Select (c => c.ToUpper())
    .Where (upper => upper.StartsWith ("T"))
```

(It omits the final **Select(upper=>upper)** because it's redundant.)

Multiple Generators

A query can include multiple generators (**from** clauses). For example:

```
int[] numbers = { 1, 2, 3 };
string[] letters = { "a", "b" };

IEnumerable<string> query = from n in numbers
                            from l in letters
                            select n.ToString() + l;
```

The result is a cross product, rather like you'd get with nested **foreach** loops:

```
"1a", "1b", "2a", "2b", "3a", "3b"
```

When there's more than one **from** clause in a query, the compiler emits a call to **SelectMany**:

```
IEnumerable<string> query = numbers.SelectMany (
  n => letters,
  (n, l) => (n.ToString() + l));
```

SelectMany performs nested looping. It enumerates every element in the source collection (**numbers**), transforming each element with the first lambda expression (**letters**). This generates a sequence of *subsequences*, which it then enumerates. The final output elements are determined by the second lambda expression (**n.ToString()+l**).

If you subsequently apply a **where** clause, you can filter the cross product and project a result akin to a *join*:

```
string[] players = { "Tom", "Jay", "Mary" };
```

```
IEnumerable<string> query =
  from name1 in players
  from name2 in players
  where name1.CompareTo (name2) < 0
  orderby name1, name2
  select name1 + " vs " + name2;

RESULT: { "Jay vs Mary", "Jay vs Tom", "Mary vs Tom" }
```

The translation of this query into fluent syntax is more complex, requiring a temporary anonymous projection. The ability to perform this translation automatically is one of the key benefits of query expressions.

The expression in the second generator is allowed to use first range variable:

```
string[] fullNames =
  { "Anne Williams", "John Fred Smith", "Sue Green" };

IEnumerable<string> query =
  from fullName in fullNames
  from name in fullName.Split()
  select name + " came from " + fullName;

Anne came from Anne Williams
Williams came from Anne Williams
John came from John Fred Smith
```

This works because the expression `fullName.Split` emits a *sequence* (an array of strings).

Multiple generators are used extensively in database queries, to flatten parent-child relationships and to perform manual joins.

Joining

LINQ provides *joining* operators for performing keyed lookup-based joins. The joining operators support only a subset of the functionality you get with multiple generators/`SelectMany`, but are more performant with local queries because they use a hashtable-based lookup strategy rather than performing nested loops. (With LINQ to SQL and Entity Framework queries, the joining operators have no advantage over multiple generators).

The joining operators support *equi-joins* only (i.e., the joining condition must use the equality operator). There are two methods: `Join` and `GroupJoin`. `Join` emits a flat result set whereas `GroupJoin` emits a hierarchical result set.

The syntax for a flat join is:

```
from outer-var in outer-sequence
join inner-var in inner-sequence
  on outer-key-expr equals inner-key-expr
```

For example, given the following collections:

```
var customers = new[]
{
    new { ID = 1, Name = "Tom" },
    new { ID = 2, Name = "Dick" },
    new { ID = 3, Name = "Harry" }
};
var purchases = new[]
{
    new { CustomerID = 1, Product = "House" },
    new { CustomerID = 2, Product = "Boat" },
    new { CustomerID = 2, Product = "Car" },
    new { CustomerID = 3, Product = "Holiday" }
};
```

we could perform a join as follows:

```
IEnumerable<string> query =
  from c in customers
  join p in purchases on c.ID equals p.CustomerID
  select c.Name + " bought a " + p.Product;
```

The compiler translates this to:

```
customers.Join (                    // outer collection
  purchases,                        // inner collection
  c => c.ID,                        // outer key selector
  p => p.CustomerID,                // inner key selector
  (c, p) =>                         // result selector
    c.Name + " bought a " + p.Product
);
```

Here's the result:

```
Tom bought a House
Dick bought a Boat
Dick bought a Car
Harry bought a Holiday
```

With local sequences, the join operators are more efficient at processing large collections than `SelectMany` because they first preload the inner sequence into a keyed hashtable-based lookup. With a database query, however, you could achieve the same result equally efficiently, as follows:

```
from c in customers
from p in purchases
where c.ID == p.CustomerID
select c.Name + " bought a " + p.Product;
```

GroupJoin

`GroupJoin` does the same work as `Join`, but instead of yielding a flat result, it yields a hierarchical result, grouped by each outer element.

The query expression syntax for `GroupJoin` is the same as for `Join`, but is followed by the `into` keyword. Here's a basic example, using the `customers` and `purchases` collections we set up in the previous section:

```
IEnumerable<IEnumerable<Purchase>> query =
  from c in customers
  join p in purchases on c.ID equals p.CustomerID
  into custPurchases
  select custPurchases;   // custPurchases is a sequence
```

NOTE

An `into` clause translates to `GroupJoin` only when it appears directly after a `join` clause. After a `select` or group clause it means *query continuation*. The two uses of the `into` keyword are quite different, although they have one feature in common: they both introduce a new query variable.

The result is a sequence of sequences, which we could enumerate as follows:

```
foreach (IEnumerable<Purchase> purchaseSequence in query)
  foreach (Purchase p in purchaseSequence)
    Console.WriteLine (p.Description);
```

This isn't very useful, however, because **outerSeq** has no reference to the outer customer. More commonly, you'd reference the outer range variable in the projection:

```
from c in customers
join p in purchases on c.ID equals p.CustomerID
into custPurchases
select new { CustName = c.Name, custPurchases };
```

We could obtain the same result (but less efficiently, for local queries) by projecting into an anonymous type which included a subquery:

```
from c in customers
select new
{
  CustName = c.Name,
  custPurchases =
    purchases.Where (p => c.ID == p.CustomerID)
}
```

Ordering

The orderby keyword sorts a sequence. You can specify any number of expressions upon which to sort:

```
string[] names = { "Tom","Dick","Harry","Mary","Jay" };

IEnumerable<string> query = from n in names
                            orderby n.Length, n
                            select n;
```

This sorts first by length, then name, so the result is:

```
Jay, Tom, Dick, Mary, Harry
```

The compiler translates the first **orderby** expression to a call to OrderBy, and subsequent expressions to a call to ThenBy:

```
IEnumerable<string> query = names
  .OrderBy (n => n.Length)
  .ThenBy (n => n)
```

The ThenBy operator *refines* (not *replaces*) the previous sorting.

You can include the descending keyword after any of the orderby expressions:

```
orderby n.Length descending, n
```

This translates to:

```
.OrderByDescending (n => n.Length).ThenBy (n => n)
```

NOTE

The ordering operators return an extended type of IEnu merable<T> called IOrderedEnumerable<T>. This interface defines the extra functionality required by the ThenBy operators.

Grouping

GroupBy organizes a flat input sequence into sequences of *groups*. For example, the following groups a sequence of names by their length:

```
string[] names = { "Tom","Dick","Harry","Mary","Jay" };

var query = from name in names
            group name by name.Length;
```

The compiler translates this query into this:

```
IEnumerable<IGrouping<int,string>> query =
  names.GroupBy (name => name.Length);
```

Here's how to enumerate the result:

```
foreach (IGrouping<int,string> grouping in query)
{
  Console.Write ("\r\n Length=" + grouping.Key + ":");
  foreach (string name in grouping)
    Console.Write (" " + name);
}
```

```
Length=3: Tom Jay
Length=4: Dick Mary
Length=5: Harry
```

`Enumerable.GroupBy` works by reading the input elements into
a temporary dictionary of lists so that all elements with the
same key end up in the same sublist. It then emits a sequence
of *groupings*. A grouping is a sequence with a **Key** property:

```
public interface IGrouping <TKey,TElement>
  : IEnumerable<TElement>, IEnumerable
{
  // Key applies to the subsequence as a whole
  TKey Key { get; }
}
```

By default, the elements in each grouping are untransformed
input elements, unless you specify an **elementSelector** argument. The following projects each input element to uppercase:

```
from name in names
group name.ToUpper() by name.Length
```

which translates to this:

```
names.GroupBy (
  name => name.Length,
  name => name.ToUpper() )
```

The subcollections are not emitted in order of key. **GroupBy**
does no *sorting* (in fact, it preserves the original ordering.) To
sort, you must add an **OrderBy** operator (which means first
adding an **into** clause, because **group...by** ordinarily ends a
query):

```
from name in names
group name.ToUpper() by name.Length into grouping
orderby grouping.Key
select grouping
```

Query continuations are often used in a **group...by** query. The
next query filters out groups that have exactly two matches in
them:

```
from name in names
group name.ToUpper() by name.Length into grouping
where grouping.Count() == 2
select grouping
```

NOTE

A where after a group...by is equivalent to HAVING in SQL.
It applies to each subsequence or grouping as a whole,
rather than the individual elements.

OfType and Cast

OfType and Cast accept a nongeneric IEnumerable collection
and emit a generic IEnumerable<T> sequence that you can subsequently query:

```
var classicList = new System.Collections.ArrayList();
classicList.AddRange ( new int[] { 3, 4, 5 } );
IEnumerable<int> sequence1 = classicList.Cast<int>();
```

This is useful because it allows you to query collections written
prior to C# 2.0 (when IEnumerable<T> was introduced), such
as ControlCollection in System.Windows.Forms.

Cast and OfType differ in their behavior when encountering an
input element that's of an incompatible type: Cast throws an
exception whereas OfType ignores the incompatible element.

The rules for element compatibility follow those of C#'s is
operator. Here's the internal implementation of Cast:

```
public static IEnumerable<TSource> Cast <TSource>
            (IEnumerable source)
{
  foreach (object element in source)
    yield return (TSource)element;
}
```

C# supports the Cast operator in query expressions: simply
insert the element type immediately after the from keyword:

```
from int x in classicList ...
```

This translates to:

```
from x in classicList.Cast <int>() ...
```

Dynamic Binding (C# 4.0)

Dynamic binding defers *binding*—the process of resolving types, members, and operations—from compile time to runtime. Dynamic binding is useful when at compile time *you* know that a certain function, member, or operation exists, but the *compiler* does not. This commonly occurs when you are interoperating with dynamic languages (such as IronPython) and COM, and in scenarios when you might otherwise use reflection.

A dynamic type is declared with the contextual keyword `dynamic`:

```
dynamic d = GetSomeObject();
d.Quack();
```

A dynamic type tells the compiler to relax. We expect the runtime type of `d` to have a `Quack` method. We just can't prove it statically. Since `d` is dynamic, the compiler defers binding `Quack` to `d` until runtime. To understand what this means requires distinguishing between *static binding* and *dynamic binding*.

Static Binding Versus Dynamic Binding

The canonical binding example is mapping a name to a specific function when compiling an expression. To compile the following expression, the compiler needs to find the implementation of the method named `Quack`:

```
d.Quack();
```

Let's suppose the static type of `d` is `Duck`:

```
Duck d = ...
d.Quack();
```

In the simplest case, the compiler does the binding by looking for a parameterless method named `Quack` on `Duck`. Failing that, the compiler extends its search to methods taking optional parameters, methods on base classes of `Duck`, and extension methods that take `Duck` as its first parameter. If no match is found, you'll get a compilation error. Regardless of what method gets bound, the bottom line is that the binding is done by the compiler, and the binding utterly depends on statically knowing the types of the operands (in this case, `d`). This makes it *static binding*.

Now let's change the static type of `d` to `object`:

```
object d = ...
d.Quack();
```

Calling `Quack` gives us a compilation error, because although the value stored in `d` can contain a method called `Quack`, the compiler cannot know it since the only information it has is the type of the variable, which in this case is `object`. But let's now change the static type of `d` to `dynamic`:

```
dynamic d = ...
d.Quack();
```

A `dynamic` type is like `object`—it's equally nondescriptive about a type. The difference is that it lets you use it in ways that aren't known at compile time. A dynamic object binds at runtime based on its runtime type, not its compile-time type. When the compiler sees a dynamically bound expression (which in general is an expression that contains any value of type `dynamic`), it merely packages up the expression such that the binding can be done later at runtime.

At runtime, if a dynamic object implements `IDynamicMetaObjectProvider`, that interface is used to perform the binding. If not, binding occurs in almost the same way as it would have had the compiler known the dynamic object's runtime type. These two alternatives are called *custom binding* and *language binding*.

Custom Binding

Custom binding occurs when a dynamic object implements `IDynamicMetaObjectProvider` (IDMOP). Although you can implement IDMOP on types that you write in C#, and that is useful to do, the more common case is that you have acquired an IDMOP object from a dynamic language that is implemented in .NET on the Dynamic Language Runtime (DLR), such as IronPython or IronRuby. Objects from those languages implicitly implement IDMOP as a means to directly control the meanings of operations performed on them. Here's a simple example:

```
using System;
using System.Dynamic;

public class Test
{
  static void Main()
  {
    dynamic d = new Duck();
    d.Quack();       // Quack was called
    d.Waddle();      // Waddle was called
  }
}
public class Duck : DynamicObject
{
  public override bool TryInvokeMember (
    InvokeMemberBinder binder, object[] args,
    out object result)
  {
    Console.WriteLine (binder.Name + " was called");
    result = null;
    return true;
  }
}
```

The `Duck` class doesn't actually have a `Quack` method. Instead, it uses custom binding to intercept and interpret all method calls.

We discuss custom binders in greater detail in Chapter 19 of *C# 4.0 in a Nutshell* (O'Reilly).

Language Binding

Language binding occurs when a dynamic object does not implement `IDynamicMetaObjectProvider`. Language binding is useful when working around imperfectly designed types or inherent limitations in the .NET type system. A typical problem with using numeric types is that they have no common interface. We have seen that methods can be bound dynamically; the same is true for operators:

```csharp
static dynamic Mean (dynamic x, dynamic y)
{
  return (x + y) / 2;
}
static void Main()
{
  int x = 3, y = 4;
  Console.WriteLine (Mean (x, y));
}
```

The benefit is obvious—you don't have to duplicate code for each numeric type. However, you lose static type safety, risking runtime exceptions rather than compile-time errors.

NOTE

Dynamic binding circumvents static type safety, but not runtime type safety. Unlike with reflection, you cannot circumvent member accessibility rules with dynamic binding.

By design, language runtime binding behaves as similarly as possible to static binding, had the runtime types of the dynamic objects been known at compile time. In our previous example, the behavior of our program would be identical if we hardcoded `Mean` to work with the `int` type. The most notable exception in parity between static and dynamic binding is for extension methods, which we discuss in the section "Uncallable Functions" on page 172.

NOTE

Dynamic binding also incurs a performance hit. Because of the DLR's caching mechanisms, however, repeated calls to the same dynamic expression are optimized— allowing you to efficiently call dynamic expressions in a loop. This optimization brings the typical overhead for a simple dynamic expression on today's hardware down to less than 100 ns.

RuntimeBinderException

If a member fails to bind, a `RuntimeBinderException` is thrown. You can think of this like a compile-time error at runtime:

```
dynamic d = 5;
d.Hello();      // throws RuntimeBinderException
```

The exception is thrown because the `int` type has no `Hello` method.

Runtime Representation of dynamic

There is a deep equivalence between the `dynamic` and `object` types. The runtime treats the following expression as `true`:

```
typeof (dynamic) == typeof (object)
```

This principle extends to constructed types and array types:

```
typeof (List<dynamic>) == typeof (List<object>)
typeof (dynamic[]) == typeof (object[])
```

Like an object reference, a dynamic reference can point to an object of any type (except pointer types):

```
dynamic x = "hello";
Console.WriteLine (x.GetType().Name);  // String

x = 123;  // No error (despite same variable)
Console.WriteLine (x.GetType().Name);  // Int32
```

Structurally, there is no difference between an object reference and a dynamic reference. A dynamic reference simply enables dynamic operations on the object it points to. You can convert from **object** to **dynamic** to perform any dynamic operation you want on an **object**:

```
object o = new System.Text.StringBuilder();
dynamic d = o;
d.Append ("hello");
Console.WriteLine (o);   // hello
```

Dynamic Conversions

The **dynamic** type has implicit conversions to and from all other types. For a conversion to succeed, the runtime type of the dynamic object must be implicitly convertible to the target static type.

The following example throws a **RuntimeBinderException** because an **int** is not implicitly convertible to a **short**:

```
int i = 7;
dynamic d = i;
long l = d;      // OK - implicit conversion works
short j = d;     // throws RuntimeBinderException
```

var Versus dynamic

The **var** and **dynamic** types bear a superficial resemblance, but the difference is deep:

> **var** says, "Let the *compiler* figure out the type."
> **dynamic** says, "Let the *runtime* figure out the type."

To illustrate:

```
dynamic x = "hello";  // Static type is dynamic
var y = "hello";      // Static type is string
int i = x;            // Runtime error
int j = y;            // Compile-time error
```

Dynamic Expressions

Fields, properties, methods, events, constructors, indexers, operators, and conversions can all be called dynamically.

Trying to consume the result of a dynamic expression with a **void** return type is prohibited—just as with a statically typed expression. The difference is that the error occurs at runtime.

Typically, expressions involving dynamic operands are themselves dynamic, since the effect of absent type information is cascading:

```
dynamic x = 2;
var y = x * 3;        // Static type of y is dynamic
```

There are a couple of obvious exceptions to this rule. First, casting a dynamic expression to a static type yields a static expression. Second, constructor invocations always yield static expressions—even when called with dynamic arguments.

In addition, there are a few edge cases where an expression containing a dynamic argument is static, including passing an index to an array and delegate-creation expressions.

Dynamic Member Overload Resolution

The canonical use case for **dynamic** involves a dynamic *receiver*. This means that a dynamic object is the receiver of a dynamic function call:

```
dynamic x = ...;
x.Foo (123);        // x is the receiver
```

However, dynamic binding is not limited to receivers: the method arguments are also eligible for dynamic binding. The effect of calling a function with dynamic arguments is to defer overload resolution from compile time to runtime:

```
class Program
{
  static void Foo (int x)    { Console.WriteLine ("1"); }
  static void Foo (string x) { Console.WriteLine ("2"); }

  static void Main()
  {
    dynamic x = 5;
    dynamic y = "watermelon";
```

```
    Foo (x);    // 1
    Foo (y);    // 2
  }
}
```

Runtime overload resolution is also called *multiple dispatch* and is useful in implementing design patterns such as *visitor*.

If a dynamic receiver is not involved, the compiler can statically perform a basic check to see whether the dynamic call will succeed: it checks that a function with the right name and number of parameters exists. If no candidate is found, you get a compile-time error.

If a function is called with a mixture of dynamic and static arguments, the final choice of method will reflect a mixture of dynamic and static binding decisions:

```
static void X(object x, object y) {Console.Write("oo");}
static void X(object x, string y) {Console.Write("os");}
static void X(string x, object y) {Console.Write("so");}
static void X(string x, string y) {Console.Write("ss");}

static void Main()
{
  object o = "hello";
  dynamic d = "goodbye";
  X (o, d);              // os
}
```

The call to X(o,d) is dynamically bound because one of its arguments, d, is dynamic. But since o is statically known, the binding—even though it occurs dynamically—will make use of that. In this case, overload resolution will pick the second implementation of X due to the static type of o and the runtime type of d. In other words, the compiler is "as static as it can possibly be."

Uncallable Functions

Some functions cannot be called dynamically. You cannot call:

* Extension methods (via extension method syntax)

- Any member of an interface (via the interface)
- Base members hidden by a subclass

This is because dynamic binding requires two pieces of information: the name of the function to call, and the object upon which to call the function. However, in each of the three uncallable scenarios, an *additional type* is involved, which is known only at compile time. As of C# 4.0, there's no way to specify these additional types dynamically.

When calling extension methods, that additional type is an extension class, chosen implicitly by virtue of `using` directives in your source code (which disappear after compilation). When calling members via an interface, the additional type is communicated via an implicit or explicit cast. (With explicit implementation, it's in fact impossible to call a member without casting to the interface.) A similar situation arises when calling a hidden base member: you must specify an additional type via either a cast or the `base` keyword—and that additional type is lost at runtime.

Attributes

You're already familiar with the notion of attributing code elements of a program with modifiers, such as `virtual` or `ref`. These constructs are built into the language. *Attributes* are an extensible mechanism for adding custom information to code elements (assemblies, types, members, return values, and parameters). This extensibility is useful for services that integrate deeply into the type system, without requiring special keywords or constructs in the C# language.

A good scenario for attributes is serialization—the process of converting arbitrary objects to and from a particular format. In this scenario, an attribute on a field can specify the translation between C#'s representation of the field and the format's representation of the field.

Attribute Classes

An attribute is defined by a class that inherits (directly or indirectly) from the abstract class `System.Attribute`. To attach an attribute to a code element, specify the attribute's type name in square brackets, before the code element. For example, the following attaches the `ObsoleteAttribute` to the `Foo` class:

```
[ObsoleteAttribute]
public class Foo {...}
```

This attribute is recognized by the compiler and will cause compiler warnings if a type or member marked obsolete is referenced. By convention, all attribute types end in the word *Attribute*. C# recognizes this and allows you to omit the suffix when attaching an attribute:

```
[Obsolete]
public class Foo {...}
```

`ObsoleteAttribute` is a type declared in the `System` namespace as follows (simplified for brevity):

```
public sealed class ObsoleteAttribute : Attribute {...}
```

Named and Positional Attribute Parameters

Attributes may have parameters. In the following example, we apply `XmlElementAttribute` to a class. This attribute tells XML serializer (in `System.Xml.Serialization`) how an object is represented in XML and accepts several *attribute parameters*. The following attribute maps the `CustomerEntity` class to an XML element named `Customer`, belonging to the *http://oreilly.com* namespace:

```
[XmlElement ("Customer", Namespace="http://oreilly.com")]
public class CustomerEntity { ... }
```

Attribute parameters fall into one of two categories: positional or named. In the preceding example, the first argument is a *positional parameter*; the second is a *named parameter*. Positional parameters correspond to parameters of the attribute type's public constructors. Named parameters correspond to public fields or public properties on the attribute type.

When specifying an attribute, you must include positional parameters that correspond to one of the attribute's constructors. Named parameters are optional.

Attribute Targets

Implicitly, the target of an attribute is the code element it immediately precedes, which is typically a type or type member. You can also attach attributes, however, to an assembly. This requires that you explicitly specify the attribute's target.

Here is an example of using the CLSCompliant attribute to specify Common Language Specification (CLS) compliance for an entire assembly:

```
[assembly:CLSCompliant(true)]
```

Specifying Multiple Attributes

Multiple attributes can be specified for a single code element. Each attribute can be listed either within the same pair of square brackets (separated by a comma) or in separate pairs of square brackets (or a combination of the two). The following two examples are semantically identical:

```
[Serializable, Obsolete, CLSCompliant(false)]
public class Bar {...}

[Serializable] [Obsolete] [CLSCompliant(false)]
public class Bar {...}
```

Writing Custom Attributes

You can define your own attributes by subclassing System.Attribute. For example, we could use the following custom attribute for flagging a method for unit testing:

```
[AttributeUsage (AttributeTargets.Method)]
public sealed class TestAttribute : Attribute
{
  public int     Repetitions;
  public string  FailureMessage;

  public TestAttribute () : this (1) { }
  public TestAttribute (int repetitions)
  {
    Repetitions = repetitions;
  }
}
```

Here's how we could apply the attribute:

```
class Foo
{
  [Test]
  public void Method1() { ... }

  [Test(20)]
  public void Method2() { ... }

  [Test(20, FailureMessage="Debugging Time!")]
  public void Method3() { ... }
}
```

AttributeUsage is itself an attribute that indicates the construct (or combination of constructs) that the custom attribute can be applied to. The **AttributeTargets** enum includes such members as **Class**, **Method**, **Parameter**, **Constructor** (and **All**, which combines all targets).

Retrieving Attributes at Runtime

There are two standard ways to retrieve attributes at runtime:

- Call **GetCustomAttributes** on any **Type** or **MemberInfo** object.
- Call **Attribute.GetCustomAttribute** or **Attribute.GetCus tomAttributes**.

These latter two methods are overloaded to accept any reflection object that corresponds to a valid attribute target (Type, Assembly, Module, MemberInfo, or ParameterInfo).

Here's how we can enumerate each method in the preceding Foo class that has a TestAttribute:

```
foreach (MethodInfo mi in typeof (Foo).GetMethods())
{
  TestAttribute att = (TestAttribute)
    Attribute.GetCustomAttribute
    (mi, typeof (TestAttribute));

  if (att != null)
    Console.WriteLine (
      "Method {0} will be tested; reps={1}; msg={2}",
      mi.Name, att.Repetitions, att.FailureMessage);
}
```

Here's the output:

```
Method Method1 will be tested; reps=1; msg=
Method Method2 will be tested; reps=20; msg=
Method Method3 will be tested; reps=20; msg=Debugging Time!
```

Unsafe Code and Pointers

C# supports direct memory manipulation via pointers within blocks of code marked unsafe and compiled with the /unsafe compiler option. Pointer types are primarily useful for interoperability with C APIs, but may also be used for accessing memory outside the managed heap or for performance-critical hotspots.

Pointer Basics

For every value type or pointer type *V*, there is a corresponding pointer type *V**. A pointer instance holds the address of a value. This is considered to be of type *V*, but pointer types can be (unsafely) cast to any other pointer type. The main pointer operators are:

Operator	Meaning
&	The *address-of* operator returns a pointer to the address of a value.
*	The *dereference* operator returns the value at the address of a pointer.
->	The *pointer-to-member* operator is a syntactic shortcut, in which x->y is equivalent to (*x).y.

Unsafe Code

By marking a type, type member, or statement block with the unsafe keyword, you're permitted to use pointer types and perform C++ style pointer operations on memory within that scope. Here is an example of using pointers to quickly process a bitmap:

```
unsafe void BlueFilter (int[,] bitmap)
{
  int length = bitmap.Length;
  fixed (int* b = bitmap)
  {
    int* p = b;
    for (int i = 0; i < length; i++)
      *p++ &= 0xFF;
  }
}
```

Unsafe code can run faster than a corresponding safe implementation. In this case, the code would have required a nested loop with array indexing and bounds checking. An unsafe C# method may also be faster than calling an external C function, since there is no overhead associated with leaving the managed execution environment.

The fixed Statement

The fixed statement is required to pin a managed object, such as the bitmap in the previous example. During the execution of a program, many objects are allocated and deallocated from the heap. In order to avoid unnecessary waste or fragmentation of memory, the garbage collector moves objects around. Pointing to an object is futile if its address could change while referencing it, so the **fixed** statement tells the garbage collector to "pin" the object and not move it around. This may have an impact on the efficiency of the runtime, so fixed blocks should be used only briefly, and heap allocation should be avoided within the fixed block.

Within a **fixed** statement, you can get a pointer to any value type, an array of value types, or a string. In the case of arrays and strings, the pointer will actually point to the first element, which is a value type.

Value types declared inline within reference types require the reference type to be pinned, as follows:

```
class Test
{
  int x;
  unsafe static void Main()
  {
    Test test = new Test();
    fixed (int* p = &test.x)    // Pins test
    {
      *p = 9;
    }
    System.Console.WriteLine (test.x);
  }
}
```

The Pointer-to-Member Operator

In addition to the & and * operators, C# also provides the C++ style -> operator, which can be used on structs:

```
struct Test
{
  int x;
  unsafe static void Main()
  {
    Test test = new Test();
    Test* p = &test;
    p->x = 9;
    System.Console.WriteLine (test.x);
  }
}
```

Arrays

The stackalloc keyword

Memory can be allocated in a block on the stack explicitly using the stackalloc keyword. Since it is allocated on the stack, its lifetime is limited to the execution of the method, just as with any other local variable. The block may use the [ ] operator to index into memory:

```
int* a = stackalloc int [10];
for (int i = 0; i < 10; ++i)
    Console.WriteLine (a[i]);   // Print raw memory
```

Fixed-size buffers

Memory can be allocated in a block within a struct using the fixed keyword:

```
unsafe struct UnsafeUnicodeString
{
  public short Length;
  public fixed byte Buffer[30];
}

unsafe class UnsafeClass
{
  UnsafeUnicodeString uus;

  public UnsafeClass (string s)
  {
    uus.Length = (short)s.Length;
    fixed (byte* p = uus.Buffer)
      for (int i = 0; i < s.Length; i++)
        p[i] = (byte) s[i];
  }
}
```

The fixed keyword is also used in this example to pin the object on the heap that contains the buffer (which will be the instance of UnsafeClass).

---

void*

A *void pointer* (**void***) makes no assumptions about the type of the underlying data and is useful for functions that deal with raw memory. An implicit conversion exists from any pointer type to **void***. A **void*** cannot be dereferenced, and arithmetic operations cannot be performed on void pointers. For example:

```
class Test
{
  unsafe static void Main()
  {
    short[] a = {1,1,2,3,5,8,13,21,34,55};
    fixed (short* p = a)
    {
      //sizeof returns size of value-type in bytes
      Zap (p, a.Length * sizeof (short));
    }
    foreach (short x in a)
      System.Console.WriteLine (x);  // Prints all zeros
  }

  unsafe static void Zap (void* memory, int byteCount)
  {
    byte* b = (byte*) memory;
      for (int i = 0; i < byteCount; i++)
        *b++ = 0;
  }
}
```

Pointers to Unmanaged Code

Pointers are also useful for accessing data outside the managed heap (such as when interacting with C DLLs or COM), or when dealing with data not in the main memory (such as graphics memory or a storage medium on an embedded device).

Preprocessor Directives

Preprocessor directives supply the compiler with additional information about regions of code. The most common preprocessor directives are the conditional directives, which provide a way to include or exclude regions of code from compilation. For example:

```
#define DEBUG
class MyClass
{
  int x;
  void Foo()
  {
    # if DEBUG
    Console.WriteLine ("Testing: x = {0}", x);
    # endif
  }
  ...
}
```

In this class, the statement in Foo is compiled as conditionally dependent upon the presence of the DEBUG symbol. If we remove the DEBUG symbol, the statement is not compiled. Preprocessor symbols can be defined within a source file (as we have done), and they can be passed to the compiler with the /define:*symbol* command-line option.

With the #if and #elif directives, you can use the ||, &&, and ! operators to perform *or*, *and*, and *not* operations on multiple symbols. The following directive instructs the compiler to include the code that follows if the TESTMODE symbol is defined and the DEBUG symbol is not defined:

```
#if TESTMODE && !DEBUG
   ...
```

Bear in mind, however, that you're not building an ordinary C# expression, and the symbols upon which you operate have absolutely no connection to *variables*—static or otherwise.

The #error and #warning symbols prevent accidental misuse of conditional directives by making the compiler generate a warning or error given an undesirable set of compilation symbols.

Here's a complete list of preprocessor directives:

Preprocessor directive	Action
`#define symbol`	Defines *symbol*
`#undef symbol`	Undefines *symbol*
`#if symbol [operator symbol2]...`	*symbol* to test
	operators are ==, !=, &&, and || followed by `#else`, `#elif`, and `#endif`
`#else`	Executes code to subsequent `#endif`
`#elif symbol [operator symbol2]`	Combines `#else` branch and `#if` test
`#endif`	Ends conditional directives
`#warning text`	*text* of the warning to appear in compiler output
`#error text`	*text* of the error to appear in compiler output
`#line [number ["file"] | hidden]`	*number* specifies the line in source code; *file* is the filename to appear in computer output; *hidden* instructs debuggers to skip over code from this point until the next `#line` directive
`#region name`	Marks the beginning of an outline
`#endregion`	Ends an outline region
`#pragma warning`	See below

Pragma Warning

The compiler generates a warning when it spots something in your code that seems unintentional. Unlike errors, warnings don't ordinarily prevent your application from compiling.

Compiler warnings can be extremely valuable in spotting bugs. Their usefulness, however, is undermined when you get *false* warnings. In a large application, maintaining a good signal-to-noise ratio is essential if the "real" warnings are to get noticed.

To this effect, the compiler allows you to selectively suppress warnings with the #pragma warning directive. In this example, we instruct the compiler not to warn us about the field Message not being used:

```
public class Foo
{
  static void Main() { }

  #pragma warning disable 414
  static string Message = "Hello";
  #pragma warning restore 414
}
```

Omitting the number in the #pragma warning directive disables or restores all warning codes.

If you are thorough in applying this directive, you can compile with the /warnaserror switch—this tells the compiler to treat any residual warnings as errors.

XML Documentation

A *documentation comment* is a piece of embedded XML that documents a type or member. A documentation comment comes immediately before a type or member declaration, and starts with three slashes:

```
/// <summary>Cancels a running query.</summary>
public void Cancel() { ... }
```

Multiline comments can be done either like this:

```
/// <summary>
/// Cancels a running query
/// </summary>
public void Cancel() { ... }
```

or like this (notice the extra star at the start):

```
/**
    <summary> Cancels a running query. </summary>
*/
public void Cancel() { ... }
```

If you compile with the /doc directive, the compiler extracts
and collates documentation comments into a single XML file.
This has two main uses:

- If placed in the same folder as the compiled assembly,
  Visual Studio automatically reads the XML file and uses
  the information to provide IntelliSense member listings to
  consumers of the assembly of the same name.

- Third-party tools (such as Sandcastle and NDoc) can
  transform an XML file into an HTML help file.

Standard XML Documentation Tags

Here are the standard XML tags that Visual Studio and documentation generators recognize:

<summary>

> <summary>...</summary>

Indicates the tool tip that IntelliSense should display for
the type or member. Typically a single phrase or sentence.

<remarks>

> <remarks>...</remarks>

Additional text that describes the type or member. Documentation generators pick this up and merge it into the
bulk of a type or member's description.

<param>

> <param name="*name*">...</param>

Explains a parameter on a method.

<returns>

> <returns>...</returns>

Explains the return value for a method.

\<exception\>

> \<exception [cref="*type*"]\>...\</exception\>

Lists an exception that a method may throw (`cref` refers to the exception type).

\<permission\>

> \<permission [cref="*type*"]\>...\</permission\>

Indicates an `IPermission` type required by the documented type or member.

\<example\>

> \<example\>...\</example\>

Denotes an example (used by documentation generators). This usually contains both description text and source code (source code is typically within a `<c>` or `<code>` tags).

\<c\>

> \<c\>...\</c\>

Indicates an inline code snippet. This tag is usually used inside an `<example>` block.

\<code\>

> \<code\>...\</code\>

Indicates a multiline code sample. This tag is usually used inside an `<example>` block.

\<see\>

> \<see cref="*member*"\>...\</see\>

Inserts an inline cross-reference to another type or member. HTML documentation generators typically convert this to a hyperlink. The compiler emits a warning if the type or member name is invalid.

`<seealso>`

```
<seealso cref="member">...</seealso>
```

Cross-references another type or member. Documentation generators typically write this into a separate "See Also" section at the bottom of the page.

`<paramref>`

```
<paramref name="name"/>
```

References a parameter from within a `<summary>` or `<remarks>` tag.

`<list>`

```
<list type=[ bullet | number | table ]>
  <listheader>
    <term>...</term>
    <description>...</description>
  </listheader>
  <item>
    <term>...</term>
    <description>...</description>
  </item>
</list>
```

Instructs documentation generators to emit a bulleted, numbered, or table-style list.

`<para>`

```
<para>...</para>
```

Instructs documentation generators to format the contents into a separate paragraph.

`<include>`

Merges an external XML file that contains documentation. The path attribute denotes an XPath query to a specific element in that file.

Index

We'd like to hear your suggestions for improving our indexes. Send email to
index@oreilly.com.

L

Related Titles from O'Reilly

.NET and C#

O'REILLY®

Get even more for your money.

Join the O'Reilly Community, and register the O'Reilly books you own. It's free, and you'll get:

* 40% upgrade offer on O'Reilly books
* Membership discounts on books and events
* Free lifetime updates to electronic formats of books
* Multiple ebook formats, DRM FREE
* Participation in the O'Reilly community
* Newsletters
* Account management
* 100% Satisfaction Guarantee

Registering your books is easy:
1. Go to: oreilly.com/go/register
2. Create an O'Reilly login.
3. Provide your address.
4. Register your books.

Note: English-language books only

To order books online:
oreilly.com/order_new

For questions about products or an order:
orders@oreilly.com

To sign up to get topic-specific email announcements and/or news about upcoming books, conferences, special offers, and new technologies:
elists@oreilly.com

For technical questions about book content:
booktech@oreilly.com

To submit new book proposals to our editors:
proposals@oreilly.com

Many O'Reilly books are available in PDF and several ebook formats. For more information:
oreilly.com/ebooks

O'REILLY®

Spreading the knowledge of innovators   oreilly.com